Creation's Heartbeat

Creation's Heartbeat

The Bible's Entry Code in Genesis 1:1

at the place of entry, the key is often hidden...

Dr Y Fass

Otto RvF

http://www.biblejolts.org

Order via http://creationsheartbeat.blogspot.com

Published by Otto RvF
PO Box 5145, Laytonsville, MD 20882, USA

ISBN 978-0-473-15781-4

Printed in the U.S.A. and U.K. by Lightning Source.

Library of Congress catalog card 2009910952

BISAC: REL006060, REL006400, REL040090

An Enquiry into the First Verse of Genesis

"The beginning of Thy word is truth..." Psalm 119:160

"This verse says nothing but 'Explain me!' " Rashi, Commentary, Bereishis

To my wife

at the place of entry, the key is often hidden...

Contents

Part 1: A Basis for Understanding

Outline	1
Gaining a Foothold	3
A Necessary Enquiry	11

Part 2: Ten Steps to Understanding

Outline	23
Step One: The Act of Creation	25
Step Two: The Burning House	37
Step Three: Family	51
Step Four: Broken Connections	63
Step Five: The Arrow	73
Step Six: The Creator's Heartbreak	81
Step Seven: The Sign	93
Step Eight: Hidden Names	103
Step Nine: The Barest Breath	113
"Here I Am": Assembling the Message	125
Step Ten: Recovering the Question	135

Part 3: Understanding Gained

Outline   145

The Entry Code   147

Conclusions   163

Shma   179

Appendices

Appendix A: The Hebrew alphabet   185

Appendix B: The twenty-six components   187

Appendix C: Objections   193

Note: Quotations from the Bible are usually taken either from the *Stone Edition Tanach*, Mesorah Publications, or *The Holy Bible: New American Standard*, Broadman and Holman. Where verse numbering differs between the two, the reference is given with a stroke, for example Hosea 14:8/9.

Other references are given in the footnotes.

Part 1
A Basis for Understanding

"I stretch beyond the bounds of the world,
I'm smaller than a worm, clearer than the moon, swifter than
the sun...
I stretch across the region of angels; I fill the earth with
myself...
Say what my name is."
Riddle 66 (concerning creation), The Exeter Book, (Anglo-
Saxon, 6th Century CE)

T he Creator of life knows how to compress, transfer and secure vital information. How might He speak to us in the beginning and how can we check our understanding of what is said? Is it possible to proceed in a methodical manner to explore the Bible's opening statement?

Part One identifies five bases for a rigorous methodology so that our enquiry is tightly focussed and proceeds within strict principles and guidelines. Ten tests for the results are specified. Using traditional Judaic techniques, we examine the first four words of Genesis to see what they tell us. The Hebrew letters are considered in the order and form that they occur; there is no shake or shuffle or number counting.

The expectations of what the opening words can reveal are set unreasonably high in this enquiry. That way, they cannot be met by human reason or by a human author.

§

Gaining a Foothold

At the place of entry, the key is often hidden. Perhaps this is so with the most ancient of books, the Hebrew Bible. If there is a message encoded in the beginning, it would be the Bible's first and most urgent message to us; the key that opens our understanding to the treasures that lie beyond. The opening words set out the first act of creation by the Creator. In a world where Creator or creation seem to have failed, do these words still have mysteries to tell; could they give us hope?

The Hebrew sages are strangely troubled by the opening words of Genesis. Do they contain a secret not to be divulged or do they tell us to bring into the open that which is hidden? How is one to read the first words anyway, and why begin with such problematic Hebrew? Clearly there is much beneath the apparent simplicity of the first verse.

Science and the mind of God

The Bible's description of creation can astonish with its many layers. The great 13th Century CE Jewish scholar Ramban deduced from it that the universe was originally contained in a tiny seed, like a grain of mustard, and then hugely expanded and changed in substance, to give rise to all matter. His explanation precedes by 700 years the 'big bang' theory of modern astro-physics which argues the same. Sir Isaac Newton held that, when properly deciphered, the Hebrew Bible and traditions contain founding knowledge of creation and the universe.[1]

The opening of Genesis describes the creation of the heavens and the earth. Maybe it also sets out a founding principle that drives the universe: a linchpin or a peg on which it all hangs. Modern science is uncomfortable with any starting point save the sovereignty of human observation and reasoning used to make deductions from the material world. Some doubt that science will ever "be able to raise the curtain on the mystery of creation". For others, the aim is, as Stephen Hawking puts it, "the ultimate triumph of human reason ... [to] know the mind of God."[2] But, perhaps we can step beyond the autonomous world of science and human sovereignty to revelation. Perhaps the mind of the Creator is already made known to us and invites us to engage, not by abandoning our faculty of reason but – as with Sir Isaac Newton – by opening it to a different source of information.

An atheist will rule out the possibility of communication from the Creator as a matter of first principle. There is nobody there, so there is nothing to hear. Instead, we seek God's first principle. If there is a Creator, how might He speak to us and how can we check our understanding of what is said? This enquiry will demonstrate that, unlike the atheist's statement, God's first principle is testable.

Only the Creator is equipped to resolve the deepest questions of creation. The human heart can react in many different ways to the Bible's claim to be a series of communications from the Creator. We may ignore it or deny, defy, or disprove it. We may shift its sense or otherwise use it for our own purposes. Through all this, and despite the difficulties of interpretation, translation and contextualization, can God possibly be heard, if He is to be heard at all?

If He speaks, can we comprehend Him? The Bible identifies the core problem: "my thoughts are not your thoughts, neither are your ways My ways", declares the Lord. (Isaiah 55:8) The traverse between

---

[1] See: Nachmanides, (known as Ramban) *Commentary on Torah,* Gen 1:4.
(Ramban lived 1194–1270, Spain and the Holy Land.) On Newton (1643–1727),
see: Goldish, Matt (1998) *Judaism in the Theology of Newton,* Kluwer. Einstein was
fascinated by this aspect of Newton's work (see his September 1940 letter to
Yahuda, Albert Einstein Archives, Hebrew University of Jerusalem).
[2] Stephen Hawking, (1998) *A Brief History of Time,* Bantam, p210. The preceding
quote is from Jastrow, Robert (1992) *God and the Astronomers,* Norton, N.Y., p107.

Creator and creation is not a matter casually to enter into. Our quest is to find a key that can lead us to the Creator's answers, even to His resolve towards humanity. But a key is concealed for a reason. To gain so great a key, what must we do and how can we prepare our understanding to grasp its message, if message there be?

Such a message would take us beyond the limitations of the material world and show us behind 'mere creation' to its purpose and its Creator. As a cosmological statement Genesis 1:1 looks safe: one can agree or not but it does not seem to matter much. By contrast, the reader may suffer from vertigo if faced with an invitation to engagement by the Creator concerning creation and its purpose. Such an encounter will have consequences.

The discussion has been hypothetical. There are many 'if's and uncertainties. These can be summed up in two questions. How can we determine whether the verse contains a hidden message of deep significance or establish the truth of what emerges? How can this enquiry proceed in a methodical way and with what guidelines and reference points to avoid speculation and minimize conjecture?

A sound foothold and a basis to review our findings are necessary. Perhaps unexpectedly for a modern mindset, these can be gained. Consider how the Creator can speak to us of that which is essential. A gram of DNA – the stuff of life – has the information content of a trillion DVDs, and has to be unpacked in a very particular way to provide life. The Creator of life evidently knows how to compress, transfer and secure vital information. If He wished, He could encode His intent for creation in less than a handful of words and reveal His own heart there to those who sought after Him.

We should expect His message to be trustworthy and to demonstrate its authority. The Creator would speak to us in a way that could penetrate through all the noise of successive generations and diverse cultures. Perhaps, He would speak at many levels and in various modes, both openly and in ways less evident. The language used, even the individual Hebrew letters, would provide resonances between the opening words and all that follows to show that they are parts of one great unity.

Precise, letter by letter, unpacking of DNA is required in order to read and apply its code to build life. Similarly, there is a way to unpack the Creator's code for creation. The enquiry focuses on the first four Hebrew words of the Bible with their unalterable primacy of place and importance in setting the scene for all that follows. It looks in meticulous detail at every component of the first part of the first verse in the Bible: Genesis 1:1. We examine each meaning or hint that can be found there. To discover the rhythm underlying its opening words, let Scripture speak for itself.

Method

What method can apply so much attention to so small a space and give confidence in the results?

The primary sense of the first verse in the Bible is conveyed by a straightforward reading and by the best translations. Can anything substantive emerge from searching more deeply into half a verse? How can it be anything more than messing around with a few words, shuffling and changing their contents, so that almost anything might come out or any meaning be attached to it? Yet there is much that can be deduced, provided we are careful in how we treat the original Hebrew. This enquiry is not far-fetched, not mere speculation, not seeking the impossible, not beyond testing, and, in much of its technique, not unusual within the Hebraic tradition. We can make such assertions and proceed with confidence for five reasons.

First, the nature of the language and discourse: The basis of Hebrew words lies in short, root words which contain the core meaning, and which then have prefixes, suffixes or 'infixes' added, or are combined together. Hebrew text is inherently poetic and multi-faceted; different meanings can be explored (sometimes playfully) in the links between root words and in the words or letters added.[3]

In Hebraic (and some Christian) thinking there is not a single superfluous phrase, word or letter in Scripture. Each is worth examination because Scripture forms an integral whole. A traditional Hebraic approach views each part of the text as connected to the unity of the whole and as contributing to one grand discourse. The occurrences of a particular word or phrase or image or type are seen in relation to its other occurrences and to the overall themes. Each part within the whole can illuminate and be illuminated by every other part.

If there is a message, then its encoding will utilise the characteristics of the Hebrew language and Hebrew Scripture. Consequently, the enquiry proceeds within a traditional form of

---

[3] The distinctives of the Hebrew language in terms of how the reader decodes its meaning and is able to identify root words and patterns are discussed in Shimron, Joseph (2006) *Reading Hebrew: The Language and the Psychology of Reading It*, Routledge.

Hebraic discourse that provides well tried methods to go deeper. This footing in the nature of the language and discourse gives a firm basis on which to proceed.

Second, in terms of traditional Hebraic discourse, we impose much more stringent rules than usual with this type of enquiry. This is discussed further in the next chapter. The enquiry remains focused on what Scripture says and minimizes speculation or the introduction of extraneous elements. This is an enquiry into, not an essay upon. To allow examination in depth, we limit the field of discussion and consequently the number of possible words and meanings to be explored.

The *third reason* is the focus on examining the detail and implications of only four specific words. These are not picked at random or on the basis of some theory. They claim primacy of attention because of their location as the first words in the Bible in the first statement about the universe. This tightly constrains the enquiry.

The *fourth reason* lies in the different approaches within this tiny canvas. To unpack and comprehend the first four words we apply four different approaches (outlined in the next chapter), going progressively deeper into the text. The restrictions mentioned apply to each approach. Collectively, these approaches provide their own cross-check on each other. If there is a message, then it should resound through all four approaches. The heartbeat should emerge with the depth and clarity of quadraphonic sound.

The *fifth reason* is the series of tests that are applied to the results of this enquiry. In combination, these ten tests are tough. We look for the results to be:

- *Inclusive:* Within the strict criteria outlined above, every element produced by applying this enquiry's method to the first four words must be considered. We do not select some findings and reject others. The results built from these findings should be comprehensive and include every component, rather than selecting some and ignoring others.

- *Precise:* Each component discovered should perfectly fit with every other component, like pieces of a jigsaw puzzle that mesh together precisely when correctly placed.

- *Coherent:* The pieces of the puzzle should combine to make a coherent whole. We seek a composition that uses all the findings in order to tell a meaningful story that is internally consistent. The story should be complete and without loose ends. Everything should be connected, though this does not mean that every matter has to be resolved.

- *Robust:* The components should reinforce each other to build the overall architecture, so that the argument depends on no single component. Its themes and main topics should emerge even when some findings are excluded: an inescapable rhythm.

- *Appropriate:* The composition emerging should be in harmony with its location at the opening of the Bible, with the creation narrative of Genesis 1 as a whole and the questions that it raises, and with the wider text of the Bible and its core themes.

- *Powerful:* The message to be read from this composition should have richness and depth of meaning: a key that unlocks all that follows.

- *Relevant:* The message should address our deepest needs and questions, not be a theological stance or goal statement.

- *Elegant:* Scientific theories are often judged by their elegance in solving seemingly complex problems. This is applying Occam's razor: the simplest solution that works is preferred, provided it takes all the circumstances into account. Complexity should be reduced to simplicity. (This doesn't require the detail behind the solution to be simple, nor its consequences!)

- *Connected* to actual events: What is revealed should be prophetic, accurate, specific, and concrete, not a dream or aspiration.

- *Unique:* There should be no other way of bringing together the components we discover that meets the other criteria set out here. This test is an invitation to the reader to challenge our results.

If the code we uncover can meet all these tests, it will indeed be both remarkable and transformative.

In sum, there is a fivefold rationale and method to search for a key or code at the opening of Genesis, including ten tests for what we find. There are guidelines on how to proceed and reference points against which to consider what emerges. We have grounds for our enquiry and can examine the key that is found to ensure that it is correctly fashioned, that it fits the lock, and that it opens the door to a great house. Nothing less will do, for the purpose is to hear from God.

From an Hebraic perspective, the basis of the techniques employed is recognizable. A *midrash* (enquiry) delves deep into the language of the Bible, according to set rules, to reveal its beauty and truth through explicating and harmonizing texts. For those coming from outside the Hebraic perspective, our enquiry demonstrates the rewards of approaching Scripture in its own terms in order to seek the truth from within its words. This contrasts with a typical Western analysis that uses an external viewpoint or standard in order to test Scripture and align it with a pre-determined philosophy or worldview. For the five reasons given, our enquiry is more rigorous, tightly focused, and less speculative than such a perspective. As with a Western analysis, the aim is to gather information and to proceed through deductive logic. But, there is less 'wiggle room' and fewer assumptions imported from outside the text in this enquiry.

Equally, mystical speculation about symbolism or numerical ciphers hidden within Genesis can meet none of the five reasons for confidence set out here. Instead of imposing an external viewpoint on the text or pursuing an inwardly focused mysticism, we use the techniques specified to draw out what the text itself says. This enquiry does not ignore possible symbols within the text, but ties them to the context and subjects them to the stipulated methodology.

Style

The enquiry proceeds on the basis that the Creator may communicate with us through the detail of Scripture and aims to search out His opening message to us. The method adopted enables the enquiry to probe deeply without risk of losing balance or focus because the search is grounded in the text.

The style this produces has three levels. First, close attention is paid to the detail of the text in order to pursue the clues provided and respond to the puzzles and challenges. To ignore the detail is to miss or misunderstand the code we seek. As with DNA, the code has to be carefully unpacked to discover the basis of life and of its reproduction. Nothing is left out or ignored. What is compressed within the opening words is unfolded and the resulting links pursued through the rest of the Hebrew Bible. The detailed evidence is accumulated piece by piece.

Second, the enquiry seeks to build a broader view of the message and weight of the Bible's opening words. Using the evidence gained, the entry code is assembled piece by piece. As the pieces fit together, a picture of increasing clarity emerges.

Third, the accumulation and assembly of findings from the two preceding levels of discussion are used to grasp the entry code as a whole and to understand what its message – the heartbeat of creation – means for us.

The style adopted has purpose. Each level requires and builds on the previous level. The combination of levels and the underpinning methodology give reasons for confidence and facilitate discussion.

The first four words of the first verse are examined by proceeding through ten steps, each of which moves mostly between the first two levels. Shifting between the detail of textual points and 'big picture' questions may produce the vertigo remarked on earlier. That is why the enquiry remains anchored by the text throughout and multiple tests are applied to our findings. It is the accumulation, assembly, consistency and rigour of evidence coming from the detail that sustains and validates a wider view.

An intricate structure with a definite rhythm, emerges within the tiny frame of four words. The lens provided through these few words will hopefully give the reader much to consider as the underlying issues of Creator and creation are raised and new perspectives gained on perhaps familiar passages in the Bible. But this is not something merely to admire or ponder or debate. This is the Bible's entry code. It speaks of creation's heartbeat. It provides the key to reflect upon and investigate the rest of Scripture, a path to understand the Creator's heart and the nature of His plan for us from first to last. It is a plan that requires action. That is why it is stated first of all.

The message sets out the basis of the reality that we experience. It speaks to each of us about our relationship with the Creator and the rest of creation. It confronts and tests us and may be hard to bear. The message is an invitation to look beyond ourselves and fully realize our humanity. The reader is invited to join a voyage of discovery that is by its nature risky, a voyage into the heartbeat of creation.

A Necessary Enquiry

What do we most need to know? Faced with the really big questions, *The Hitchhiker's Guide to the Galaxy* tells us that the answer is forty-two. Although fun, this cannot engage us. It voices a modern despair and solves nothing because nothing can be solved. The opening of Genesis invites us to go far beyond. The finite mind cannot expect to grasp God's purpose for creation but perhaps here in the beginning there is a key that is given to us. To know the Creator's purpose and plan would give us the basis for understanding both the physical universe and our own internal moral world. It could tell us the heartbeat of creation and perhaps explain our own heartbreak.

This is a necessary discussion. The opening words may seem an austere statement of cosmology: "In the beginning God created the heavens and the earth." Yet this verse says nothing but "Explain me!" according to the famous Judaic commentator Rashi, whilst Maimonides forbids the divulgence of its mysteries.[4]

---

[4] Rashi, lived in Troyes, France, 1040–1105, Maimonides in Spain and Egypt c1135–1204. See: *Rashi's Commentary: Bereishis* and Maimonides *Moreh,* Preface to Part III. Maimonides is commenting on a passage in the *Talmud – Hagigah* 2:1 – which places limits on open discussion of the creation account. *Beresheith Rabbah* 1:10 understands the same passage as saying that we are to go forward from the

There is no riddle older than these words at the beginning of the Bible, whose layers of meaning no translation can begin to suggest. To quote a leading, contemporary rabbi: "The story in the first part of the Book of Genesis is very well known and still it remains a secret."[5] What might this book of books, story of all stories, tell us in the beginning, and dare we look?

Unreasonable expectations

Let us set our expectations of what the opening words of Genesis can reveal to us unreasonably high. That way, our expectations cannot possibly be met by the human reason of a human author. We cannot trust a human author to get behind creation to its purpose or to its Creator.

What could our unreasonable expectations be? The opening statement of the Bible must speak profoundly. Suppose those few words pose and answer the core question of all existence, their message addressed to each of us. We might hope for a promise of history summed up, the essence and crisis of existence grasped, even the key to its resolution supplied, or maybe a hint of the end to all things. If written by the supreme Deity, we could dare to seek all of that captured in a few words: the key for all creation. And these words we unreasonably expect must speak in a way that is understandable and testable by human reason.

Our purpose is to discover the heartbeat of creation within the opening words of Genesis, the book of origins. This enquiry aims to provide reason and method and cause for reflection on creation and our place within it.

One of the founders of modern Western discourse, Immanuel Kant, states that:

---

opening letter of Genesis, and not enquire into what is above or below or before that. (*Beresheith Rabbah* is a *midrash* on the book of Genesis from the 4th–6th Century CE.) In practice, other great Judaic sages, such as Ramban, have not interpreted the *Talmud* as excluding them from writing on the deeper aspects of creation. The early text *Sefer Yetzirah*, possibly from the 2ndC BCE, is devoted to discussing the creation of the world. Lurianic Kabbalah (16thC CE onwards) speculates about "before creation".

[5] Rabbi Adin Steinsaltz quoted in Goldberg, Hillel (2000) "Genesis, cosmology and evolution", *Jewish Action,* Summer, p1. Steinsaltz (born 1937 in Jerusalem) was for a time appointed President of a reconvened Sanhedrin.

> Two things fill the mind with ever new and increasing
> wonder and awe: the starry heavens above and the moral
> law within.   *Critique of Practical Reason,* Conclusions.

Perhaps they can be united by beginning at the beginning. To be fully human is to be both of the dust (Genesis 2:7) and in the image of God (Genesis 1:27).

This enquiry applies neither the telescope to scan the skies, nor the inward eye to search within ourselves, but the magnifying glass to look more closely at what the words say. With this glass, we are not looking for minutiae. We pursue the big picture hidden within these words by considering their component parts, the consistencies and oddities that are revealed, and what emerges as the parts are brought together.

Entertaining as riddles may be, this is more: we are embarking on a spiritual voyage. Although covering only four words, the voyage is testing, even dangerous. The reader will come upon a deep puzzle, a succession of clues, and contradictions that challenge us to resolve them. As we proceed, the clues begin to cohere together and lead toward a complete yet simple solution, a solution with direct implications for each of us. The key turns and the door opens.

There are two questions for the reader:

- A proposition for the mind: Is this message contained within Genesis 1:1? How can this be and what light does it throw on what follows?

- A proposition for the heart: Is this significant: does it speak to our deepest need and to the pain and suffering of our world?

The opening words of Genesis are necessarily fixed in their location as the entry point to the whole book. They have inescapable primacy of place. Jewish sages such as the Vilna Gaon teach that the first time a word or letter appears in the Bible is its spiritual home, the place that tells us how to understand its depths.[6] The first appearance is the key. We are invited to search for that key to unlock what is said.

The first four Hebrew words provide the key that we seek, so this enquiry does not go beyond them. They speak of the act of creation and the remaining words of the opening phrase speak of that which is created: the heavens and the earth. To examine the material nature of creation is not essential to the present enquiry. There are sufficient

---

[6] Based on a remark in the *Talmud, Baba Kamma* 55a. The Vilna Gaon lived 1720–1797 in Vilna, Lithuania.

pieces to solve the puzzle without going beyond the first four words when looked at in the context of the *Tanach* as a whole. These words reveal a design that is woven throughout the *Bible*.

Let us search for the Creator's viewpoint by a relentless focus on the precise words and letters used at the beginning of the book. If this is the word of God, then it is His description of His creation and His worldview. To understand creation, we need to grasp what He says rather than attempt to assimilate His view with ours.

That something is hidden in the beginning is no surprise. The Hebrew word *olam*, meaning the 'universe' or 'eternity', comes from a root which means 'concealment' or 'hiding'. Here is a hint of something concealed about the nature of the universe or eternity.[7] As this is inherent to the act of creation, we can expect it to be so at the beginning of creation and time, something hidden within the Bible's first verse.

Beneath the surface

Scholars have long known that the Bible provides a series of hints *(remazim)* and secrets *(sodot)*. The text calls upon us to search out matters as far as we can. Some things remain secret: "The secret things belong to the Lord our God, but the things revealed belong to us" (Deuteronomy 29:29). But, with diligence, much can be brought to light by those who search for riches: "It is the glory of God to conceal a matter, but the glory of kings is to search out a matter." (Proverbs 25:2) There comes a time for such matters to be spoken of.

Debate is ongoing as to the precise meaning of the first words in Genesis. The grammar itself is obscure. However, our aim is to look beneath the surface of the grammar. Many are the modes of examination of the Bible but this enquiry sticks with the simplest and most ancient. Our enquiry is into the first few words and their component parts to discover what they can tell us when examined in Hebraic terms. It is tightly focused, based on tried methods, and subject to a tough combination of tests. The five aspects of this technique were laid out in the first chapter. We place the highest demands on it and the results are startling.

---

[7] Some rabbis hold that an essential aspect of the Creator is to be hidden; for example Solomon Luria (1534–1572 or 1510–1574; Egypt and the Holy Land). The *Talmud Hagigah* 12a says that light by which one can see "from one end of the universe to the other" is concealed in the *Torah* (the first five books of the Bible).

To decode the first four words, we explore beyond the immediate sense of these words, just as one would with any poetry or prose of quality. Because of the way the *Tanach*, the Bible, is written in the original Hebrew, the letters and words have layers of meaning which cannot be captured in translation. The opening words show us what to look out for later in the Bible. They alert us to ideas and themes that reoccur in the Bible and they illuminate and deepen our understanding of these. We can both be informed by the wider Bible and that wider reading can be informed by our discoveries in Genesis 1:1.[8] This is a dialogue with the text.

Hebraic technique are utilised to look for the sense of Scripture at a number of levels: the surface level, the hint, the search and the hidden level. There have been abuses and sharp disagreements within this traditional form of Hebraic discourse. These give cause for caution, but not for abandoning this mode of discourse, otherwise no approach could stand. In addition to the nature of the language and discourse, four other reasons for confidence in our method were outlined in the opening chapter: the stringent rules applied (more stringent than normal as we shall see); the tight focus on just four words whose primacy is given by the Bible itself; the different approaches adopted to the text (discussed shortly); and the ten tests deployed which, in combination, provide a rigorous check on the results.

The aim is to be accurate and thorough in unfolding what is set out there, in accordance with strict rules. Such restrictions help ensure that it is the words and their author who speak to us, not we who speak our imaginings into the words. The reader will judge which is the case here. The enquiry proceeds by building "precept upon precept" (Isaiah 28:10) to arrive at a solution.

Discipline is needed to delve into the *Tanach*. The rules are strict in order to give confidence that what is found is significant and not the product of scanning through multiple combinations of letters or other possibilities looking for results that fit a desired picture: 'torturing the data' as it is called. We require the key to fit precisely for our aim is to learn what God is saying to us in the beginning, not to engage in speculation.

The enquiry looks solely at the letters and words as they are written, with the spelling and word order as they are written in the Hebrew Bible. It looks only at words found in the Bible in the form and with the meanings used there. Within the given order of words, we

---

[8] This approach is exemplified in *Beresheith Rabbah*. See, for example 1:6.

will consider words contained within words. For example, the Hebrew word translated "in the beginning" contains within it in the correct order the Hebrew letters for the word for creation. This we will look at. We will consider the accepted connotations of individual Hebrew letters if there is a tight, logical connection between the letter concerned and the word(s) adjacent to it.

Unlike some rabbinical studies, we do not take the beginnings or endings of successive words and add them together or use reverse orders of letters or words, or change the order of letters. For example, it has been argued, that God placed His seal upon the first three words of the Bible because their final letters, *tav-aleph-mem*, when re-arranged, give us *aleph-mem-tav*, the Hebrew word for truth.[9] This we do not look at. Nor does the enquiry substitute one letter of the alphabet for another, similar looking or sounding, one. Nor does it examine the numerical value of individual letters or groups of letters in order to locate patterns and meanings not evident on the surface.[10] Such approaches have proved perennially fascinating because they generate much material that can be constructed into various forms and used to prompt debate and reflection. By contrast, we will be looking at the Hebrew letters that are there in the first four words and in the order and form that they occur to see what they may tell us. There is no shake or shuffle or number counting.

Our search will be based on the *Tanach*, the Hebrew Bible, sometimes referred to as the Old Testament. Within this, the first five books are called the *Torah*, the Law. The enquiry will also use:

- the *Targums* (translations of the Hebrew Bible into Aramaic, possibly originating before the Common Era, and given high status in Judaic commentaries)

- the *Talmud* (comprising the 'oral law' or traditions transmitted by the ancient Hebrew scholars, eventually in written form, and discussions around these)

- various *midrashim* (detailed enquiries into the *Talmud*) that are widely acknowledged for their wisdom

---

[9] This popular argument may originate with Rabbi Simcha Bunam (Poland, 1767–1827).
[10] The thirteen rules of interpretation developed by Ishmael ben Elisha (1st–2nd Century CE) are widely accepted within Judaism, and we operate within them. The thirty-two rules attributed to Yoseph HaGalili (a near contemporary) widen to include other techniques, such as those mentioned in the preceding paragraph. These we do not follow.

- further Judaic and other interpreters of more recent times, up until the present

- supporting material such as lexicons.

Only works that are well known and highly respected will be utilized, along with occasional illustrative material. Inevitably, there are debates and disagreements about, between and within these sources. Between them, these different resources help piece together the full significance of Genesis 1:1. These are the tools of our research.

We will learn the views of many Hebraic scholars over many centuries on the critical issues that are raised. This is more than a matter of studying different perspectives on the first chapter of Genesis. The lens of this enquiry will provide a focus to consider commentaries and debate on many questions. Some debates may be unfamiliar or comments surprising. Each can inform our explorations and provide a range of ideas and perceptions against which to check our understanding of what the opening words tell us. Throughout, the focus remains on the message of those words themselves. We have a framework to place them within and to test the conclusions drawn.

Beneath the surface of the text lie a series of hints, allusions and prompts. As these are brought to light, any particular finding could be shrugged off as unclear or uncertain. This is rather like discovering an isolated archaeological remnant during an excavation: not a lot of weight can be put on it. Some findings or pointers are no more than fragments. But the results build up step by step and fit together consistently. In combination they become increasingly powerful, the connections between them more and more difficult to put aside. We can begin to grasp the broader construct to which they belong. As with an archaeological excavation, we must carefully assemble the disparate pieces uncovered within stringent limits and see if together they construct a coherent picture. It is the combined weight of evidence that convinces.

First we need to dig deep. We are not undertaking an archaeological dig but the excavation of the opening words of the book of the books. The Jewish sage Maimonides states:

> The basic fundamental and the pillar of all wisdom is to know that there is a first cause, that brings into being all that is. And all that exists, in heaven and earth and all that is between them, only exist because of the truth of His being.
> *Mishneh Torah, Hilchos Yesodei HaTorah*, 1:1.

Our understanding of this truth affects our understanding of all else, including who we are.

Ten steps

The enquiry will focus on the first four Hebrew words, one of which cannot even be translated into English. It proceeds through each word in turn, looking at its constituent parts, sometimes letter by letter. (The Hebrew alphabet is set out in Appendix A.) This examination leads us through a sequence of ten steps:

Step 1   *The Act of Creation*
The beginning of the beginning. The word for creation, the absolute distinction between Creator and creation, and its deep and terrible implications.

Step 2   *The Burning House*
The first word; first deliberation. Two different cuts that explain the 'how' of relationship between Creator and creation. The basis on which we can enter into relationship with God, but its precarious nature.

Step 3   *Family*
The first word; second deliberation. A further cut that demonstrates the 'why' of relationship. The potential for closeness between humanity and God. Our hope for its renewal.

Step 4:   *Broken Connections*
The first word; third deliberation. A final way of dividing the first word which shows the 'what' of relationship. Giving and receiving. Forging close relationship between Creator and creation.

Step 5   *The Arrow*
The second word. The nature of God's continuing creative engagement with His creation. His plan for history.

Step 6   *The Creator's Heartbreak*
The third word by which the Creator is made known. The 'who' of the relationship in terms of the role He plays. The cost of His engagement.

Step 7 *The Sign*
The fourth word which leads to the bridge between Creator and creation and to *Elohim's* all encompassing sign to us.

Step 8 *Hidden Names*
The hidden names within the first four words that encapsulate and express what has gone before and speak of the Creator's loving kindness.

Step 9 *The Barest Breath*
Two threads woven through the design. One speaks of the presence of God and the other speaks of a surprising absence.

Step 10 *Recovering the Question*
A final component that tells of the hand of the Creator, of His image and of finding our identity there.

These steps take us through the first four words in the Bible in conformity with the method and criteria set out in the preceding chapter. They can be grouped into four distinct stages:

- Step one considers the implications of the verse as a whole and of the act of creation.

- Steps two to seven proceed through each word in turn, examining individual components within these words.

- In the eighth step we look at ways of reading the first four words in combination.

- In steps nine and ten we consider recurrent letters that run throughout the first four words and reveal more of their underlying rhythm.

Each stage adopts a different approach. Together, the four different approaches help us to unpack and comprehend what the first words have to say from a multi-dimensional perspective.

Each step focuses on distinct details as part of the process to reveal what lies within the four words. Through these steps, we find twenty-six separate components. These are subject to the tests set out previously. Step by step, a consistent rhythm and a coherent set of questions and emphases emerge. A composition with a clear message unfolds through the logic embedded within the first verse. This leads us to the entry code and its message. The result must then be considered as a whole to see if it makes sense both to mind and to heart: can it meet our unreasonable expectations; can it fully resolve the profound problem posed by the text; and can it do so in a way that is significant to us?

We all look for answers that fit within a frame of reference that is convenient to us. We all bring our own biases and limitations. Yet, truth can still be found if we are prepared to listen, for the Creator is able to communicate with us through His word. This enquiry searches within the text for meaning by letting the words speak for themselves. As the book of Proverbs says, Wisdom cries out to be heard "at the entrance of the gates of the city" (1:21). Let us search for her "as for hidden treasures" (2:4). Let us begin at the gateway to the book, and hear the first thing God has to say to us so that we can discover His frame of reference rather than a reflection of our own. That way, we can "arrive where we started and know the place for the first time."(T S Eliot, *Four Quartets, Little Gidding, V*)

To prepare for our voyage, three points:

First, Hebrew reads from right to left, unlike Latin scripts such as English, which read from left to right. Hence, in this document, the English translations and letter by letter transcriptions run from left to right whilst the Hebrew runs in the other direction.

Second, many vowels and some other differences in sound (for example between an 's' sound and a 'sh' sound) are not shown by distinct letters. Instead, a system of 'pointings' – little dots and dashes placed around the letters – has developed to show the vowels and mark the differences in pronunciation. These pointings were absent from the original scrolls of the Hebrew Bible. Ancient Hebrew is a little like a modern 'txt msg' or 'twitter' and can be equally terse! We have omitted the pointings from our discussion.

Third, the original Hebrew text does not have the chapter and verse divisions that assist navigation of most printed Bibles, nor full stops or commas or spaces between words. For ease of reading, these features have been retained.

Rashi asks a strange question: why does the Bible begin as it does rather than with the first commandment given to the children of Israel, which does not occur until well into the book of Exodus, the second book of the Bible.[11] Rashi focuses on the relationship between God

---

[11] Rashi, *Commentary: Bereishis.*

and Israel, maintained through commandments and instructions. Why not begin with these, as they are what Israel most needs to hear?

As we shall see, the Bible does begin by establishing the basis of our relationship with God. This is no soft, comfortable message:

> "Is not my word like fire?" declares the Lord, "and like a hammer which shatters a rock?"   (Jeremiah 23:29)

Rather, it confronts our preconceptions about God and our connection with Him.

Our explorations will show that the first four words in the Bible contain astonishing depths, subtle allusions, hints, and layers of meaning. It will take focus and precision to decipher the puzzle and to absorb the significance and implication of those few words. They do not readily yield up their significance to a casual glance or first reading. Here, as elsewhere, the Creator wishes us to press in and to pay careful attention. What emerges is an intense and stark message, never more relevant than in the modern age, a beacon placed at the doorway to the book.

Part 2:
Ten Steps to Understanding

"...those who diligently seek me will find me." (Proverbs 8:17)

T he first verse of the Bible tells us to bring into the open that which is hidden. It unlocks the basis of the moral order that is integral to the nature of creation and sets its heartbeat.

In no other account is there a being who completely transcends all of creation and who simply speaks things into existence. The universe is presented as the product of a single, creative will. To explore the first verse is to explore the nature and resolution of the consequent divide.

Part Two pursues this by investigating every aspect of the first four words that fits within the criteria of this enquiry. Each of twenty-six components yielded by these words is examined. We look at the verse as a whole, its constituent elements, alternative ways of reading it, and pattern of letters within it.

The reader is challenged by the text, with its dualities and dilemmas and its call for our engagement. There is a shadow in the beginning and hint of a resolution. Step by step, the pieces of the puzzle are assembled. Twin themes emerge to provide a coherent and recurring message. They point to a history and plan for creation.

Genesis 1:1 reveals a potential harmony between Creator and creation which hinges on the answer to a profound question.

§ §

Step One: The Act of Creation

The beginning of the beginning. The word for creation, the absolute distinction between Creator and creation, and its deep and terrible implications.

I mmovable, locked in place, hiding in plain view: the opening words of Genesis cannot be overlooked. The reader of the Bible, the *Tanach*, will read at least these words and the scribes will not err in replicating them. These words have been carefully transmitted and studied over the millennia. They provide the foundation for all that follows.

Let us begin our journey at the proper place, at the beginning. Here, in stark terms, the Bible sets out the basics of who we are and who God is. There is a Creator and there is the creation that He created; simple, yet hard to grasp. As a modern Jewish writer states, "There is a tension between the benevolent clarity and power of the narrative and the acknowledgment of mystery that inheres in the very first word and that develops as the implications of the beginning are realized."[12]

In step one, we glimpse the outline of this mystery. Folded within the opening words is a statement about the foundation of creation. Step by step, a powerful and unexpected statement is unfolded, a vast

---

[12] Zornberg, Avivah G (1996) *The Beginning of Desire: Reflections on Genesis,* Doubleday, N.Y., p4.

claim about the nature and purpose of creation. These first words tell
us what we most need to be told. They state and resolve a mystery and
speak prophetically of what is to come. In order to find, first we have
to search and to listen, to search out the "apples of gold in settings of
silver" (Proverbs 25:11).

In his commentary on Genesis, Samuel Raphael Hirsch argues that
the different Hebrew root words associated with the word *barah*
('created' or 'create' or 'creating') denote "striving to get out" or
"bringing something out into the open".[13]   A proper reading of the
opening verse of the Bible teaches us that our job is to discover and
uncover, to help bring into the open that which is hidden. The key is
waiting to be discovered and placed in the lock.   And there are
consequences for each of us.

Component a: the first sentence

The first component of our enquiry is the first verse taken as a whole.
Genesis 1:1 reads: "In the beginning God created the heavens and the
earth." The original Hebrew is (reading from right to left):

a)
$$\text{בראשית ברא אלהים את}$$
$$\text{השמים ואת הארץ}$$

←

This can be pronounced as: *BereSHEITH barAH EloHIM et
hashaMAH-yim ve'ET ha-ARetz*. A literal translation would be: "In
beginning created [or creating] God the heavens and the earth."

The entire universe came into existence a finite time ago by the
creative action of God. No other holy writings – except those derived
from the Bible – make such a claim. Even a leading humanistic Bible
commentator, offering a "new interpretation", describes the opening of
Genesis as "a shock … the very notion of a wholly omnipotent deity
was a new departure … pagans … could not imagine the gods creating

---

[13] Hirsch, Samuel Raphael, (trans.: I. Levy) (1999) *Commentary on the Torah,
Volume 1, Bereisheith / Genesis,* Judaica Press, p47. Hirsch lived mainly in
Germany and Moravia, 1808–1888.

the cosmos without a good deal of effort."[14] Instead of wrestling, there is harmony.

A core matter is established by Genesis 1:1: in the beginning was the act of creation by God. This makes an absolute distinction found in no other creation account between Creator and creation. In other creation accounts, an initial God or gods procreate with each other, expel earth from their body, or whatever. They do not transcend creation. In no other account is there a being who completely transcends all of creation and who simply speaks things into existence without effort or struggle. In Genesis alone amongst creation accounts does the Word of God have such power to create. The universe is presented as the product of a single, creative will.

Because of Genesis 1, the emphasis on the Creator God is distinctive of Judaism, Christianity, and Islam. The 'people of the book' are the people of the first verses of the book. The rabbinical scholar Ramban argues that the Torah begins with the narrative of the creation because creation is the root of Jewish faith. His near contemporary Maimonides says "He who does not believe this... denies the essential and basic principle of [Biblical] religion."[15] There is similar emphasis by major Christian theologians.[16]

The Jewish sage Rashi disagrees. He emphasises relationship as the root of faith. Maybe both Ramban and Rashi are right. As we shall see, the opening words of Genesis intertwine creation and relationship.

Our focus is on the first four words, looking letter by letter:[17]

בראשית ברא אלהים את

The four words are:

בראשית   *Beresheith*   in beginning

---

[14] Armstrong, Karen (1990) *In the beginning: a new interpretation of Genesis*, N.Y., p10-11.

[15] Maimonides, *Guide for the Perplexed*, II, 27.

[16] Zwingli, a founding father of Protestant Christianity, gave primary emphasis to the distinction between Creator and creation, whilst Luther claimed to have been the only person to have correctly understood the first chapter of Genesis (*Lectures on Genesis, chapters 1–5*). The Catholic theologian Thomas Aquinas has been termed "Thomas of creation" because of his stress on the importance of creation (G K Chesterton in his biography of Aquinas).

[17] The Judaic commentator Rabbi Bahya (Spain, 11thC) suggests that there should be a full stop after the first three words. However, as we shall see, the little fourth word adds to the first three.

בָּרָא	*Barah*	created
אֱלֹהִים	*Elohim*	God, or the Lord
אֵת	*Et*	[un-translatable word]

This looks simple enough: the Hebrew equivalent of the English translation. But there is much that cannot be captured by translation and much that requires careful exploration and consideration.

The first word, *beresheith*, can be translated as "in (or from) the beginning". In the Masoretic tradition of writing Torah scrolls, the individual letters of this first word in Genesis are widely spaced out or stretched. This invites the reader to contemplate the depth of meaning contained here more than in any other word in the Bible.[18]

Close consideration is also invited by the form of the word. The precise Hebrew form *beresheith*, typically translated as "in the beginning", is not repeated elsewhere in the *Tanach*. In other passages where the same or similar English wording is used, the original Hebrew differs. The Hebrew form *beresheith* is odd and its precise connotation in this context is unclear. Unless the author of Genesis begins the book with a slip in grammar, the writer is drawing attention to the word and the difficulty in understanding the nature of what it is talking about.[19]

The first word – *Beresheith* – begins with a B, the Hebrew letter *bet*. The *bet* is written extra large. Normally in the *Tanach* the first letter – even of a book – is written the same size as the other Hebrew letters. Only three other books in the Bible begin with an enlarged letter (Proverbs, Song of Songs, 1 Chronicles). The enlarged *bet* of *Beresheith* draws attention to itself.

בְּרֵאשִׁית

---

[18] See *Masseket Soferim*, an 8th Century CE, or earlier, treatise.

[19] This has led to dispute amongst scholars about exactly how to understand the opening verse in relation to the rest of Genesis 1. Is it a dependent or independent clause? Does it mean "In the beginning God created..." or "In the beginning of God's creating..."? This does not affect our argument and so we do not pursue the matter here.

Why begin with the letter *bet* not the letter *aleph*, the first letter of the Hebrew alphabet? Could not God arrange to begin His book with an A, an *aleph*? That seems more appropriate and more perfect. Instead:

בּ not א

Hebrew writers have debated why the letter *bet* and not the letter *aleph* begins the Bible.[20] *Elohim*, meaning 'the Lord', is the 3rd word in the opening passage and begins with *aleph*. The *Tanach* begins with the creation *(barah)* by the Creator *(Elohim)*. *Bet*, as the first letter of the Hebrew word for creation, is the appropriate opening to a book that focuses on creation.

Unlike its English translation, the Hebrew Bible begins not "In the beginning God" but "In the beginning the act of creation". God introduces Himself with the third word, *Elohim*, <u>after</u> the beginning of creation. Hirsch remarks that He can be called *Elohim* only after the creation of the world because that name refers to His relationship to the world.[21] Hence, the central issue of the whole book from its first word is the nature of that relationship.

In the first of his thirteen principles of faith, Maimonides states that creation came into being as an expression of the Creator's will and continues to be dependent upon Him: "He causes them to exist and they exist only because of Him." A recent commentator remarks:

> It is perhaps easy to imagine [a] lofty deity as long as we place him in heaven. But in the Hebrew Bible God does not remain wholly transcendent, locked into the celestial sphere. He enters human history and becomes inextricably involved with humanity.[22]

We cannot, as created beings, understand God outside of His connection with His creation. It follows that this is basic to understanding creation. To try to understand ourselves or the world outside of that is the beginning of error. The nature of relationship between Creator and creation is the very essence of understanding.

Genesis immediately makes its own claim to authority. Only by following this account can we begin to rightly know God and the world that He has created, and thus ourselves and our purpose. Genesis is

---

[20] A popular view is that the big B of Genesis 1:1 represents a big blessing *(bracha)* over creation.

[21] Hirsch, op cit., p3.

[22] Armstrong, op.cit., p13.

not the story of humanity slowly discovering – evolving – its own knowledge of God by ourselves. If it was, the opening statement is utterly misplaced in being so absolute.

Component b: the word for create

The first three Hebrew letters in the Bible form the word for 'create', *barah*:[23]

b)   בראשית

בְּרָא   *bet-reish-aleph   Barah*

The word *barah* is contained in *beresheith*, although the two words are pronounced differently and the origin of the word *barah* is different from that of the word *resheith* (beginning). The six Hebrew letters that begin the Bible and constitute the word *beresheith*, "in the beginning" already contain the word for creation. Creation is contained in the beginning (the first word) and is also the second full word in the Bible that follows *beresheith*.

This provides an underpinning statement about the nature of reality. If creation is in the beginning, there is no beginning before creation. Time begins with creation and we cannot look before that. From the beginning there is the Creator and there is the creation and there is the utmost divide between the two.

We can use the terms 'create', 'creation', and 'creativity' rather freely for everything from this first act of creation to drawing a picture or baking a cake. The Bible is not so casual in using the word *barah* in terms of God's actions. The word is used with precision and in a way that gives it huge weight. *Barah* has the sense of creation from nothing as distinct from making or forming something from something else. Even in the creation account in Genesis, God mostly makes and rarely creates.[24]

---

[23] The same three Hebrew letters – *bet-reish-aleph* – can, with different emphases in the vowel sounds, provide a root word which means 'fatness' or 'abundance', perhaps illustrating the abundance of creation. As this word is not used with the spelling *bet-reish-aleph* in the Hebrew Bible, it falls outside our rule of only referring to word forms and meanings that occur there.

[24] See, for example, Rashi on Genesis 1:14.

The root word *barah* (creation) is used in Genesis 1 of the creation of the heavens and the earth, of His creation of animal and fish life – that is, of creatures – and of His creation of man and woman. Verse 27 of Genesis 1 tells us that man is created in God's image. This is a unique distinction and a special bond between humanity and the Creator.[25] God's creative action is mentioned once each for the heavens and for the earth and for animate life, but three times for mankind. There is no doubt what the pinnacle of His creation is: human beings. Every one of us is created in His image. We are a unique combination of the dust of the earth and the breath of God.

We need to identify a basis for relationship with our Creator if we are created in God's image. There are three facets to this:

• we seek relationship with our Creator (though we may deny or be unaware of the nature of our own search)

• He seeks relationship with us

• in order to understand ourselves and the world we live, we need to understand our role in this relationship.

The opening verse directly addresses all three facets. The second facet may seem surprising but is central to the Bible's worldview. The 20thC Jewish philosopher Abraham Joshua Heschel entitles one of his books: *God in Search of Man: a Philosophy of Judaism.*

Genesis 1:28–30 and 2:15 and Psalm 8 make clear that humanity is God's agent and is responsible for the dedication of creation to its Creator. Humanity is not to be passive before the rest of creation or worship it; nor can we treat it as if it belongs to us or is at our disposal. Our position calls us to action based on our position as the pinnacle of creation; there is a partnership with the Creator.[26] This is not confined to the locality of planet earth. The setting is the creation of the heavens and the earth: all of creation.[27]

If creation is a messenger of God's mind and intent,[28] what is the message? The creation story of a culture provides its moral framework for it speaks of its foundations and worldview: how things got to be the

---

[25] Maimonides sees this as the characteristic of man that differentiates him from the animals (*Guide for the Perplexed*, 1.1). See also step ten of this enquiry.

[26] *Talmud Shabbat* 10a. Also *Kohelet Rabbah* 7.13 (a c8th C CE *midrash*).

[27] Both *shmayim* (heavens) and *eretz* (earth) are used in a variety of senses in the Bible. At its opening, they are generally understood to be used in the widest possible sense, referring to all that comes into existence.

[28] Hirsch, op.cit., p44.

way they are and the consequences for how we should act now. The book of Genesis provides such a framework. It does this in terms of the three facets just outlined. The first verse unlocks the basis of the moral order that is integral to the nature of creation itself. This sets the heartbeat for all of creation and, in particular, for us.

The duality

The letter *bet*, which begins the Genesis account, is the second letter of the Hebrew alphabet and carries the numerical value of two. Hebrew sources comment on the number of twos involved in the creation and ongoing story line of the Bible: two genders, two trees, two tablets and so forth. The Creator and His creation are the fundamental duality. This is reflected in the letter *bet* at the beginning of the creation story.

Genesis 1:1 poses the fundamental problem of this inescapable duality. This enquiry will show that the same few Hebrew words explain precisely how the Creator resolves this duality: solves what might seem unsolvable even for the Creator. It will show how this solution – hidden in the beginning – is the beginning of our own story and relationship with Him. As the duality is fundamental to creation, so must its resolution be fundamental. If there is such a solution, then it must be embedded in the nature of the Creator's first creative act where the duality is introduced. It belongs in Genesis 1:1.

How can the moral framework set by Genesis work across the great divide between Creator and creation? Necessarily the solution speaks to humanity's problems. As the pinnacle of creation, humanity straddles that divide in some sense, but how is that? We are to act with and for God but in and as part of His creation. Where do we belong?

As His creation, we are absolutely distinct from the Creator. Maimonides insists:

> There is no similarity in any way whatsoever between Him and His creatures; that His existence is not like the existence of His creatures, His life not like that of any living being, His wisdom not like that of the wisest of men, and that the difference between Him and His creatures is not merely quantitative, but absolute.[29]

The result is a fundamental tension between:

---

[29] Maimonides, op.cit., I, 35.

- humanity as the pinnacle of God's creation and in God's image, with the associated danger that we will try to make ourselves as God, and

- humanity as part of creation and separate from our Creator, with the associated danger that we will reduce ourselves to be merely another part of the created world.

At either extreme, we evade responsibility as the pinnacle of God's creation and the connecting point. The tension threatens a tear in the fabric of creation.

An Hebraic commentary says, "If God created man it is because he was not content with the angels and the beasts".[30] We are in God's image so we can reflect that image; we are to be "the candle of the Lord" (Proverbs 20:27). We can also mar that reflection. Contrast, for example, Psalm 82:6 "You are gods (or angelic), and all of you are sons of the most high" with Psalm 49:12 "But man in his pomp will not endure; he is like the beasts that perish." The duality of Creator and creation becomes a duality within humanity: we are pulled toward the Creator, yet limited by our created nature.

We strive for unity. Ideas of building a better world by our own efforts, or of the planet or biosphere evolving to higher levels by themselves, can try to remove God from history and to end the duality. The notion of humanity discovering and releasing our own potential by ourselves is powerful in today's world, including within Judaism and Christianity. The creative power of the Creator is made irrelevant or becomes defined as part of creation or a projection of our own powers. Genesis 1:1 shifts its sense to become: "In the beginning, human beings created a God who was the First Cause of all things..."[31] Unity is achieved by us or by other forces at work within creation. The distinction between Creator and creation is washed away.

Humanists have correctly identified monotheism and the concept of the Creator God as the enemy of their view of progress and evolution. It follows that the argument advanced here on our ongoing need for relationship with God is unacceptable to a purely humanistic

---

[30] *Beresheith Rabbah* 14:3, 4.

[31] Attributed to Wilhelm Schmidt (1911) by Karen Armstrong at the opening of her 1994 book *A History of God.* The English Romantic poet Shelley (1792–1822) earlier wrote of "the mind of the creator which is itself the image of all other minds" in his *A Defence of Poetry.* These views may stem from a Kabbalistic view that God's identity was shattered in creation and is now being pieced together in a process of becoming through human activity.

view. God's creative activity described in Genesis 1 provides both a moral framework for all that follows and the point of division with humanism. Humanism necessarily operates within a closed system: the realm of what has been created. It is limited to that realm, however wide or vaunted the vision. By contrast, the Genesis account points to that openness which comes from He who is not created and is beyond creation. If the Creator seeks us, then that openness both invites and challenges us.

Duality lies at the heart of the Bible's first verse. In a Biblical worldview it cannot be wished away or evaded. To deny that is to put forward a different framework and a different view of the nature of our existence. The stakes are high. A quest for unity through denial of the duality has immediate and direct implications on our outlook and on our understanding of who we are.

If the Creator is not banished altogether, He becomes a secondary – maybe imaginary – character in our story. He may be cast in the role of a good, modern parent – in the background, sympathetically facilitating us to achieve our potential – or a wicked, old-fashioned parent who quashes us with rules and punishment. Or maybe He is an absent parent, busy elsewhere. Communication with such a parent is either not possible, or not welcome, or not necessary.

The Genesis account puts forward a totally different kind of parent. The Creator continues His creative involvement with us out of concern for us and because humanity needs it; there is some lack or insufficiency on our part. We cannot lift ourselves up by our own boot straps, however much we make stuff or do stuff or pursue high minded objectives. Human history bears sad witness to this. Affinity with Him is needed for us to represent Him, to unify the duality, and to fulfil ourselves through fulfilling our role in creation. Hence:

> all other philosophical and political questions (i.e. issues of meaning and power) are subordinated to the fundamental issue of the relation of the creator and creation.[32]

Genesis 1:1 is the first communication across the divide.

To recognise the divide is the beginning of wisdom. As we shall see, the duality of Creator and creation forms the rhythm of creation's heartbeat, though in an unexpected manner.

---

[32] Bruegeman, Walter (1982) *Genesis: Interpretation*, Atlanta, p12.

God is not dead to those who are not dead toward Him. The *Tanach* holds a vital and ongoing two-way relationship between Creator and creation to be the source of our significance and purpose. Consequently, to seek this is vital to our fulfilment. By contrast, our own endeavours to build ourselves up or recreate our world make Him dead to us. When they are not centred on relationship with Him, the result of such actions will be failure towards God, towards the rest of creation, and towards ourselves.

How can we bridge the divide and access the creative power of God, if that is still at work in the world? Where can we look to find Him – if He can be found – and to find ourselves? The B, the Hebrew *bet*, tells us. Its shape directs us forward into Scripture, not looking up, down or back.[33]

 ב

It tells us to read the book.

---

[33] See *Talmud, Hagigah* 2:1. The form of the *bet* in the Proto-Sinaitic script from which the Hebrew alphabet is thought to have developed was that of an open, upright container. So, we can look into Scripture as containing all of creation.

Step Two: The Burning House

The first word; first deliberation. Two different cuts that explain the 'how' of relationship between Creator and creation. The basis on which we can enter into relationship with God, and its precarious nature.

I f there is a bridge, it looks tricky to cross. As the pinnacle of creation, humanity's relationship with our Creator is unique. It stems from conscious decision and free will.[34] How then are we, as a conscious decision, to approach the Creator? Deuteronomy 6:5 states "You shall love the Lord your God with all your heart and with all your soul and with all your might." Within a few verses, we are instructed to "fear the Lord your God" (Deuteronomy 6:2, 13 and 24). Maimonides notes the tension between love and fear when we think about an all-powerful God.[35] The opening words tackle this issue head-on as we shall see.

The Bible's opening letter ‏ב‎, the B or *bet*, stands in Hebraic thought as a symbol for the house, in this case God's house. The letter is open on one side, showing that the house is open. From the beginning, God's house is open. Openness characterizes a system where the Creator continues to be engaged with us.

We associate a house with family, as in a child's painting. But who is in this house? Step two starts to show how there can be relationship

---

[34] *Mishneh Torah, Hilchos Teshuvah*, 5.
[35] Maimonides, op.cit., 2.2.

between Creator and humanity and its nature. We begin to see the 'how' of relationship with God.

At first, the picture is vague: various dots and a few lines possibly connecting them, so to speak. Any attempt to assemble them as parts of a coherent message may seem speculative. As we look at more components, the dots and possible connecting lines increase in density, forming clusters and patterns, and the picture starts to fill out. The reader can test for themselves the rigour of the eventual results.

Component c: beginning

Beresheith, consists of *resheith*, meaning 'beginning' or 'first fruits', and the letter *bet* which means 'in'. Hence, "in the beginning":

c)   בראשית

ראשית *Resheith*

Resheith is used in the sense of first fruits to refer to Israel in Jeremiah 2:3: "Israel was holy to the Lord, the first *(resheith)* of His harvest."

Some Judaic commentaries see the verse as showing that it was for the sake of *Torah* (the first five books of the Bible) and of Israel that God created the heavens and the earth.[36] Such ideas may seem fantastical to a modern mindset. However, looking more closely at the first word, we can glimpse a definite plan and purpose for creation by the Creator. The idea of first fruits in the Bible contains the concept of a return or reciprocity for the action of the one who originally did the planting. The Creator is interested in the fruit from His creation. That is why He undertook it to begin with.

Resheith is used of the sacrifices in the temple that were to be the first fruits of the harvest. These first fruits were given as the first and best portion of the crop and to stand for the whole of the crop. They were offered back to the Creator. The rest of the harvest could then be enjoyed: it was freed by the sacrifice of the first fruits.

The theme of sacrifice will keep reoccurring within Genesis 1:1. This might seem disturbing or outmoded today, but the Bible spends time on the subject. We need to understand what its appearance here

---

[36] See *Beresheith Rabbah*, and *Seder Eliyahu Rabbah* (a 10th Century CE *midrash*); also Rashi on Genesis 1:1.

in the beginning is telling us and if and how it connects to later usages. Otherwise, something vital about the nature of creation may elude us.

Throughout the *Tanach,* the idea of first fruits is used particularly in terms of new beginnings or restorations for Israel, for example when Israel first entered the Promised Land, or when the temple was restored under Nehemiah and Ezra.[37] Genesis 1:1 fits with this since it is about the first beginning. Later, there are new beginnings or re-commencements and the purpose of the sacrifices in the temple was in part to start afresh, to clean the slate.

The use of the word *resheith* links the beginning in Genesis 1:1 to the need for new beginnings. The implication is that something goes astray meantime; otherwise there would be no need for a fresh start. This alerts us to look ahead for new beginnings in the Bible, and to the offering of first fruits to achieve this.

Israel is not only the first fruits but also the first born (Exodus 4:22). Both terms are used of Reuben, the eldest son of Jacob (who himself was renamed Israel). God does not ask for the sacrifice of the first born child, bur rather their dedication to Him. A substitute is provided for the offering of the first born, just as, when Abraham went to sacrifice his eldest son Isaac, a ram caught in a thicket was provided in Isaac's place.

As the heavens and the earth are themselves the first fruits of creation, and as Israel is the first born, how are they to be dedicated to the Creator? If there is to be a sacrifice, how is it to be made from the first fruits of all creation or of Israel? The root word *barah* (creation) can also mean 'cut down'.[38] Does creation itself or Israel have to be cut down to satisfy God? Genesis 1:1 provides an alternative path.

There is another aspect to *resheith.* The word is used in the context of wisdom in Proverbs 8:22ff:

> From everlasting, I [wisdom] was established, from the beginning *(resheith)*, from the earliest times of earth.

Wisdom founded the earth (Proverbs 3:19) and, logically, wisdom is alluded to by *resheith,* the first word in the Bible. In Judaic

---

[37] See Leviticus 23:10; Deuteronomy 26:2, 10; 2 Chronicles 31:5; Nehemiah 10:37 and 12:44; Ezra 20:40 and 48:14.

[38] It is used in this sense in Joshua 17:15 and 18 and Ezekiel 21:24 and 23:47. There is no direct connection to the cutting of a covenant – discussed under component (f) – in such usage.

understanding, wisdom denotes the *Torah*, the word of God.[39] *Torah* is to be found in the beginning. Its wisdom can tell us how to solve the problem of sacrifice.

This enquiry proceeds by looking both behind the words that can be found within Genesis 1:1 and for connections between them and with other Scriptures. The possibilities are sketched and, for the present look vague. As the findings accumulate, the results should become more robust and we can also apply the tests of inclusiveness, precision and coherence to them.

Component d: the head

Resheith comes from the word *rosh*, meaning 'head' or 'first'. The word *rosh* is contained within *resheith*:

d)   בראשית

ראש   *reish-aleph-shin   Rosh*

From the beginning there is a head.[40] With the addition of the letter *yod* this head becomes 'my head'. Here is the Creator's head for all creation.

ראשי

At the beginning of His creating, the Creator has appointed His head. *Rosh* is also used in the sense of the summit of a mountain and in Psalm 118:22 to identify the cornerstone of the temple.

Who might this head or summit or cornerstone be? The letters of *beresheith* will give us some clues. The head necessarily plays a key role in creation. We must explore further to determine what this is.

The head is critical by virtue of both the location and meaning of the word. The head in Genesis 1:1 is seen by some sages as pointing to the cornerstone or foundation of the temple and the point from which

---

[39] See: *Ben Sira* 24:23 (2nd Century BCE); *Talmud, Pirke Avoth* 3:14; the *Targums* and *Beresheith Rabbah* on Genesis 1:1. The *Talmud* states "But for the *Torah* heavens and earth would not endure." (*Pesahim* 68b)

[40] In the Proto-Sinaitic script, the form of the letter *reish* was the left profile of a man.

God began creation.[41] The Maharal of Prague teaches that the use of the Hebrew word here depicts not only the beginning of creation but also its purpose: that which creation is leading towards.[42]

Thus, *rosh* looks both forward as well as back to the beginning. *Rosh* is used many times in the *Tanach* to mean the sum total of something. The use of *rosh* here points towards that which is the summation of creation, its foundation and purpose, that which encompasses it all. In the vastness of creation, locating the head can provide a reference point or anchor for all that follows.

The letters *reish-aleph-shin*, which spell *rosh*, can also have a different and almost opposite meaning to head. Extreme poverty or destitution is usually written:

רוש   *reish-vav-shin*

It can also be written with a *yod* or an *aleph* in place of the *vav*.

ריש   *reish-yod-shin*   or   ראש   *reish-aleph-shin*

In Hebrew the letter *vav* – which tends to be weak – is dropped. In the case of the word for extreme poverty, we find instead the "frequent insertion of the vowel letter *aleph*" in its place, producing *reish-aleph-shin*.[43] Hence, in the Hebrew Bible, the word for destitution is sometimes written with the same letters as the word for head, though pronounced slightly differently. (We will return in step nine to the *vav* that is missing here, as from elsewhere in the first verse.) From the head and purpose of creation, we stumble into destitution.

Immediately, in the beginning we have struck a problem. Destitution threatens the head of creation or is somehow embodied in the creation project. The head becomes associated with destitution through the substitution of the *aleph* for the *vav*. This substitution is the cause or trigger for the movement between headship and destitution. But what is destitution doing here; surely, destitution cannot be the purpose of creation or of its head?

---

[41] *Talmud Yoma* 54b and Nachmanides on Genesis 1:1. See also footnote 131 on Isaiah 28:16.

[42] *Gevuros Hashem* 12. The Maharal of Prague lived 1520–1609.

[43] Harris, R Laird et al (Eds.) (1980) *Theological Wordbook of the Old Testament*, Chicago. The word is written with the *aleph* at 2 Samuel 12:1 and at Proverbs 6:11; 10:15; 13:23; and 30:8.

Component e: the house

If the letters forming *rosh* (head) are removed from *beresheith*, then *bet-yod-tav* is left:

e) **בראשית**

בית *bet-yod-tav* Beth

The word *beth* means 'house', just as the letter *bet* on its own can symbolise a house.

The word for house and the word for head are associated. As with other cases where we 'skip' some letters, they are not just set aside. The association between the skipped letters and the letters that bracket them will be examined. They should form an organic whole for the skip to be accepted as meaningful to this enquiry.

In this case, the word *beth* encloses the word for head. Therefore, the head is in the house and this house, in turn, is in the beginning. Given its location, the house is necessarily God's house. Within the vastness of creation we have found both a head and a house that the head inhabits. We have found, so to speak, a home.

In the Bible, the house of God refers to the temple. We cannot explore the rich symbolism of the temple here but have already seen that *rosh* (head) can be read as the cornerstone or foundation stone of the temple. Essentially, the temple is the place of sacrifice and the place where God draws closest to man. Various passages in the *Tanach* use architectural images for creation and the completion of creation is linked to the completion of the temple in some *midrashim*.[44]

The house of God, His temple, provides both a place for God to live amid His creation and a place for His creation to approach Him: a meeting place. The temple image emphasises the connection between Creator and creation. It makes God both immediate – He is with us in His house – and remote: He can only be approached through the temple's ceremonial sacrifices, priests, and formal procedures.

---

[44] *Pesikta Rabbati* 6 (8th Century CE collection of homilies) and *Pesikta De-Rav Kahana* 5b–6a (5th–6th Century CE collection of *midrashim*). Job 38:4ff; Psalm 18:15; and Psalm 104:3 use architectural images for creation and many scholars have recognized temple imagery in the description of creation. *Midrash Tanchuma Bechukotai* 3 (9th Century CE) sees the temple as fulfilling God's desire for a dwelling place in the "lower worlds".

The house of Genesis 1:1 is the house of creation, the house that God built (Isaiah 66:1–2). Since creation is troubled, one could say that this is a troubled house. The *Talmud* tells the story of a traveller who saw a burning mansion and said "Is it possible that the mansion is without someone responsible?" The owner looked out and responded "I am the owner of the mansion." This is compared to Abraham saying "Is it possible that the world is without someone responsible?" God looked out and responded "I am the master of the world." [45] As we shall see, there is fire in the house of creation, but the head of the house is present: there is a master.

We have found the head of the house who is its cornerstone. The house is the temple, a place to come near God and for sacrifice. The next two components help to unfold these connections.

Component f: covenant

As we have mentioned, the Judaic commentator Rashi asked why the Bible does not begin with the first commandment. The commandments are what Israel most needs to hear and give the basis for relationship through covenant with the Almighty. Genesis begins otherwise. However, within the first verse of Genesis we find that relationship is directly addressed. If we take the first two and the last letter of the first word, *Beresheith,* we obtain *berit (bet-reish-tav)* which means 'covenant' in Hebrew.

f) בר אש ית

ברית *bet-reish-yod-tav* *Berit* or *Bereith*

Component (g) will return to the skipped letters in the midst of covenant – the *aleph* and the *shin* - for they are integral to the Biblical view of covenant. First, let us look at covenant itself.

To modern ears, 'covenant' sounds like a particularly grand and binding kind of legal document with extra lawyers, fancy words and elaborate seals. What has this to with establishing relationship?

We should not be surprised by the appearance of covenant at the heart of creation. The seven days of creation in Genesis culminate in

---

[45] *Beresheith Rabbah,* 39:1.

the day of rest, *Shabbat*. In Judaic thinking, this is understood as the wedding ring or seal of God's covenant with Moses and Israel made when God presented the Law and the Ten Commandments to Moses on the mountain top. Keeping the Law was to be Israel's side of that covenant. When Israel is referred to as the people of God, the context is covenant (e.g. Exodus 19:5–6; Deuteronomy 7:6–9). The Law is called "the Book of the Covenant" by Moses (Exodus 24:7). Those who observe it are "sons of the covenant".[46] The Ark of the Covenant is the Holy of Holies placed at the heart of the temple by Solomon. The assembly of all Israel is usually held in the context of receiving or fulfilling covenant.

These references show that covenant is the ground for relationship with God. Consequently, those who reject God's commandments have no basis for relationship with God.[47]

The Bible contains numerous examples of covenants, both between God and man and between man and man. Scholars have found covenant arrangements in major documents from the ancient Middle East which has led them to agree with Judaic tradition that the entire book of Deuteronomy in the Bible is a covenant document, with the Ten Commandments at its core. [48]

Covenant is a means for establishing relations where there is no previous basis or over-arching framework. We might think of covenant within the context of an over-arching legal system that has a government and judicial system to make, interpret and enforce laws. By contrast, in a pre-modern society there may be no such over-arching system, no shared and underwritten framework of reference for establishing relations. Different tribal groups who come into contact with one another can establish a positive basis for relationship through gifts or the exchange of pledges or hostages. However, the full development of covenant as a basis for relationship between humanity and God appears to be restricted to the Bible and traditions deriving from it. [49] Covenant is the basis of law making, not its product.

---

[46] *Talmud, Baba Kamma* 9b, and *Gittin* 23b.

[47] See, for example, *Sifra Vayikra Nedabah*, 2.3 (an early *midrash* quoted in the *Talmud*).

[48] See, for example, Kline, Meredith G (1963) *Treaty of the Great King: the Covenant Structure of Deuteronomy*, Grand Rapids. One writer states "The entire world view of the Bible ... is built around the covenant idea." Elazar, Daniel J (1998) *Covenant and Polity in Biblical Israel: Biblical Foundations & Jewish Expressions*, Transactions, London; p64.

[49] For tribal societies, see, for example, Sahlins, Marshall (1972) *Stone Age Economics*, London. For the uniqueness of the Biblical tradition, see Elazar, op.cit.

Where there is not a close connection between parties, covenant provides a basis for relationship through making mutual and binding obligations. Relationship and obligation are tied together. Covenant binds together different parties in the same way as if they were of one blood. Covenant is to be kept regardless of circumstances. In Deuteronomy the God of Israel refers to keeping covenant and keeping His oath with Israel and with her forefathers. That is the basis of their being His chosen people.

Binding relations are not voluntary. As the 17th century political writer Thomas Hobbes puts it, "Covenants without the sword are but words and of no strength to secure a man atall."[50] In the Bible, covenant making requires the shedding of blood. The covenant is 'cut'. This refers to the cutting up of animals or cutting of one's own flesh to seal the covenant in blood. Each party makes solemn and binding oaths or undertakings to the other based on the shedding of blood. Such is the seriousness of breaking a covenant that the blood of the original offering is on the head of the covenant breaker.

By means of blood, parties are brought into close relationship such that they can trust each other. They hold obligations to meet the terms of the covenant toward each other and for each party to protect the other as if they are family members.

In the *Torah*, covenant keeping is a matter of life or death. Blood sacrifice is required to maintain the covenant if its terms are broken. Hence, the ongoing sacrifices in the temple. Leviticus 17:11 states "it is the blood by reason of the life [in it] that makes atonement."[51]

The first Passover illustrates the matter of life and death. At the culmination of the ten plagues on Egypt, the angel of death "passed over" (spared) the households where the blood from the sacrifice of a lamb was smeared on the doorposts and lintel, but killed the first born of the households that lacked that mark (Exodus 12).

The Hebrew word for sacrifice, *korban*, means literally 'to bring close'. The sacrifice and oath bring the parties to the covenant close together. Covenant makes family and provides the basis for kinship, even between God and humanity. This is a different mindset to the Greek or contemporary Western outlook of a common humanity with natural, human rights that exist of themselves with nothing done to

---

[50] *Leviathan*, II, XVII.
[51] Those making the blood sacrifice must seek to align themselves with the covenant. Sacrifice as an excuse or cover for continuing, deliberate breaches of the covenant is an abomination (Isaiah 1:15–17; Micah 6:6–9). The Lord delights in loyalty rather than sacrifice. (Hosea 6:6).

earn or sustain them. By contrast, the covenant itself defines the rights and the obligations. Only by coming into the covenant, with the associated shedding of blood and obligations, can rights be established.

In the *Talmud* the existence of creation is said to be contingent upon Israel accepting the *Torah* and accepting covenant with God.[52] This centrality is recognised in Christian thinking as well. One influential contemporary Christian writer says "creation exists to be a place for the covenant that God wants to make with man".[53]

Covenant is central to relationship with God and thus to creation. It is a moral tie based on mutual promise and obligation. Hence, covenant based morality is central to God's plan for creation. Moral failure produces the need for sacrifice in order to maintain covenant.

With that background, we can now briefly consider the main expressions of covenant between God and His creation described in the Bible. Can we identify links between the Genesis 1:1 reference and any of these? Without going into details, here is a list of the four great statements of covenant between God and humanity in the Bible:[54]

The Covenant with Noah is promised in Genesis 6:18 and specified in Genesis 9:8–10. It is a covenant with every living creature that a flood will never again destroy the earth. The rainbow is its sign or seal. The death of all animal life outside Noah's ark is the covenant sacrifice.

The Covenant with Abram (later called Abraham) is outlined in Genesis 15 & 17. This covenant concerns both land and the multiplication of Abraham's offspring. It is reiterated to his son and grandson Isaac and Jacob (Genesis 26:4 & 24; 28:14 and 35:9–12). Circumcision is its sign or seal (Genesis 17:10). In Genesis 15:10 animals are cut in two as a sacrifice to mark the covenant which God fulfils for both Himself and Abraham by passing between the divided halves of the sacrifice in the form of a smoking oven and a flaming torch (Genesis 15:17).

The Covenant with Moses, or the Mosaic covenant, is introduced in Exodus 19 and 20. The book of Deuteronomy is a setting out of the covenant document in the most elaborate and formal statement of covenant in the *Tanach*. The covenant is given amid smoke and fire on

---

[52] *Talmud, Shabbat* 88a.

[53] Pope Benedict XVI, as Ratzinger, Joseph Cardinal (Trans.: J Saward) (2000) *The Spirit of the Liturgy*, Ignatius; San Francisco, p25.

[54] For brevity, we do not discuss the priestly covenant, the covenant with David or the land covenant, each of which (arguably) may be viewed as a sub-set of the covenant with Moses. The priestly and the Davidic covenants are primarily forged with an individual family or group within Israel, though having wide implications.

the mountain top. Sacrifices are inaugurated to mark and sustain it and to cleanse Israel from her failures to keep it. The covenant is with Israel and its sign or seal is the Sabbath. It is renewed various times: Deuteronomy 29; Joshua 24; 2 Chronicles 15, 29 and 34; Ezra 10; Nehemiah 9.

The New Covenant is set out in Jeremiah 31:31–34 and described as being in the future: "Behold, days are coming..." (Jeremiah 31:27) and as an everlasting covenant. The covenant is with the house of Israel and is explicitly distinguished from the Mosaic covenant (v32) "not like the covenant which I made with their fathers... My covenant, which they broke." We are not told how this is to be fulfilled or what sacrifice will initiate or maintain it, or the nature of its sign or seal.

God initiated each of these statements of covenant. We may seek Him but He seeks us more, and He does so through covenant. The God of Abraham, Isaac and Jacob is the God of the covenant affirmed with Abraham, then with Isaac, then with Jacob. Covenant is His method of bridging the gulf between Creator and creation to build relationship with us. Each expression of covenant is sealed and sustained by sacrifice(s) that are determined by God.

Which statement of covenant is indicated in Genesis 1:1 or is it something different or more encompassing? In what way is the Creator making Himself known to us through this first mention of covenant? The reference must cohere with all that follows in the *Tanach*.

Component g: fire and foundation

In discovering *berit* – the word for covenant – within *beresheith*, two letters were omitted. When we examine these, a connection can be seen between the idea of covenant in Genesis 1:1 and the great covenants that are made between God and humanity later in the Bible. The letters in the midst of covenant – *aleph-shin* – form the word *esh*:

g)   בר **אש** ית

אש   *aleph-shin   Esh*

Esh in Hebrew means 'fire' or 'flame'. With the addition of the following *yod* this becomes 'my fire' or 'my flame'. There is fire in the house of creation.

In the middle of covenant we discover God's fire. This fits. In both the Abrahamic and Mosaic Covenants, the covenant sacrifice was consumed by fire. Fire was in the middle of the covenant, and so it is here in Genesis 1:1.

The fire in the initial forging of these two covenants came from God. It was His fire and the visible sign of His presence. Under the temple's sacrificial system, a fire was always kept burning at the altar of offerings (Leviticus 6:6/9) as a visible sign to all of God's presence. The other elements of the sanctuary or temple were not visible to the people as a whole. This fire must be His fire. In Leviticus 10:1–3 the sons of Aaron, the high priest, offer "strange fire" (that is their own fire, prepared by them outside of the arrangements of the covenant) before the Lord. In consequence, the sons are consumed by the fire. Though shocking, this demonstrates that only His fire will suffice for covenant relationship with Him. And we have found 'His fire'.

Under the Mosaic covenant, offerings are made at the temple to maintain the covenant and when there has been any failure by the people as a whole or by an individual to keep its terms. The sacrifice requires the death of the offering and its burning. Fire is the visible sign of God's presence in the covenant and of its sealing. No wonder that in the first word of Genesis His fire is found in the midst of covenant and maintained in the temple or house of God. The presence of the house of God in the opening word is not merely a piece of imagery. Its purpose is to house the covenant fire and sacrifice.

Eshy can also mean 'my foundation' (a contraction of a longer Hebrew word for foundation) and is so used of the foundation of the temple in the book of Ezra. Creation provides a temple, a place for God to come close to His creation, and its foundation is identified with the fire that consumes the covenant sacrifice. Under component (d), we saw that the head can also be seen as the cornerstone of the temple or of all creation. Through *beresheith*, that cornerstone is associated with the fire and foundation of the temple.

Both His foundation and His fire are in the midst of the covenant. The word for beginning *(beresheith)* consists of the word for covenant *(berit)* combined with the word for fire or foundation *(esh)*. If we remove covenant *(berit)* from the beginning *(beresheith)*, then His fire remains. Without covenant, there is fire in the beginning. God is compared to a consuming fire in the Bible (Exodus 24:17,

Deuteronomy 4:24 and 9:3) and the *Torah* or Law is described as fiery in Deuteronomy 33:2. The word *bara* (creation) can itself be read as meaning 'cut down'. Even in the beginning God's creation faces imminent destruction. It may be cut down; the house itself may burn.

For us not to be consumed requires covenant relationship. Covenant contains fire, just as the word *berit* contains the word *eshy*. The fire consumes the offering instead of all of creation. Therefore, creation needs that sacrifice and that fire. How these matters are arranged may lie with the head of the house where all this occurs.

Summary: the burning house

Step one showed us the deep conundrum posed by the act of creation. There is the Creator, there is creation and there is the need for relationship between the two to fulfil the purpose of creation. All else is a path to futility. But how can there be affinity across so great a divide: with what form and on what basis?

With step two, we find that, in the same breath that the division is specified, a solution to that divide emerges: the 'how' of relationship.

The appearance of the Hebrew word for covenant at the beginning of the Bible points to its central significance. It precedes even the appearance of the heavens and the earth which are the products of the first act of creation. Covenant serves to bridge the divide between Creator and creation. It is how the Creator makes Himself knowable to us. At the same time, covenant imposes ferocious obligations upon us. The tension between love and fear is heightened.

In this first deliberation upon *beresheith*, we have found a house, the temple of His presence. It is God's open house and meeting place. Within this house there is a head or cornerstone who is also associated with destitution. There is fire in the house and all of creation is threatened. Within the house, headship, sacrifice, and covenant are woven together. Sacrifice is the penalty that symbolically stands in the place of a party to the covenant, so that the party does not have to die in order to seal or maintain covenant. This thread of sacrifice and covenant will reoccur as the enquiry proceeds.

The first word in the Bible hints that the Creator provides a basis for covenant relationship through a sacrifice sealed by fire that stands for all humanity and all creation. In this way, covenant and sacrifice are joined in order to provide relationship. The fire consumes the sacrifice, rather than the whole house of creation and creation is preserved.

Wisdom, the word of God, is in the beginning. The beginning points to the first fruits of creation and the need for fruitfulness.

In examining each component within the first word, a dictionary based procedure would, for example, note that the word *esh* means 'fire' or 'foundation'. In addition, this enquiry looks at the way the word is deployed later in the *Tanach* to discover that the word *esh*, both in the sense of fire and of foundation, is used in connection with covenant. That association parallels the intertwining of the word *esh* and the word *berit* ('covenant') here in *beresheith*. Each side of that connection between *esh* and *berit* can then inform the other, providing a rich picture. By applying this technique, much can be unfolded, whilst remaining firmly based in the *Tanach*.

The second step knits together some intriguing strands, but leads to more questions. The covenant basis to relationship does not sound cosy. The fire threatens creation. What is the nature of the sacrifice and how can that be sufficient for all? Who is the head of the house and what precisely is his role? How can the head and purpose of creation be associated with destitution?

The multiplication of questions and issues could indicate that we are on the wrong track; maybe there is nothing substantive to be found by our method, only shadows. Or, as the enquiry is pursued, the questions and issues may align and point towards a simple resolution. Such a result, if it can be attained within the rules set for the enquiry, would itself affirm the validity of this enquiry's method. The richness of the story emerging from only our first deliberation upon the first word is remarkable or else it is an illusion.

Step Three: Family

The first word; second deliberation. A further cut that
demonstrates the 'why' of relationship. The potential for closeness
between humanity and God. Our hope for its renewal.

How can we dare talk of kinship with the Creator? Yet, this is
what He seeks. If the Creator seeks family relationship with us
across the great divide, then that must be why creation is precisely the
way it is. To quote an unexpected source: "It would be very difficult to
explain why the universe should begin in just this way, except as the act
of God who intended to create beings like us." (Stephen Hawking).[55]

Creation is troubled: there is a deep divide and the house is
burning. Can this be what the Creator intended? He is engaged with
His creation and the *Talmud* remarks that the Bible begins with an act
of loving kindness when God clothes Adam and Eve.[56] The previous
step showed an act of loving kindness alluded to even earlier in the
beginning. This step will reveal more about the closeness of
relationship between the Creator and humanity, the peak of His
creation. It is all about family.

Each of us is introduced to and learns about close relationships
through our own family. Family is our ideal – or less than ideal – type
where bonds of kindness and love and closeness can be modelled to us,

---

[55] (1998), op.cit., p133–134. Hawking's argument, of course, takes a very different
direction to our own.
[56] *Talmud, Sotah* 14a.

or fail to be.   Likewise, the *Torah* provides us with a model of relationship with the Divine.

The closeness of marital or family relations is based on separation from others: the marriage partners are separated to each other and family comes first. Where this does not occur, then closeness and unity is lost.   Closeness entails obligations and trust, loss as well as gain. With God these obligations are set out in the form of covenant, which is the basis for trust. The covenant is not the total of the relationship, anymore than the marriage contract is the marriage.   It provides the basis and frame for the relationship.

There might seem to be a discord between the concept of covenant and that of family. The formal obligations and ritual sacrifice of covenant contrast with the ideal of warm, intimate family relations where obligations do not need to be spelt out or calculated. Yet in marriage vows and in the bringing up of children, mutual obligations arise and deep hurts can arise in consequence. The covenants that God forms with Israel are not distant ones, like formal treaties with a king. The relationship is one of gratitude and moral obligation and the Mosaic covenant is a form of marriage contract.   Man and wife are to cleave to each other (Genesis 2:24), and the same concept of cleaving *(deveikut)* is applied to our relationship with God (Deuteronomy 10:20, 11:22, 13:4 and elsewhere).

That covenant is intertwined with *chesed* (acts of loving kindness) underlies much of the book of Jeremiah and is re-stated elsewhere.[57] Throughout the Bible, the *chesed* of the Lord is expressed through covenant and is everlasting (Psalm 103:17, Psalm 136).

As shown in the preceding step, sacrifices are required to maintain covenant, reflecting its moral character. This may seem contrary to the idea of a loving, family relationship.   The temple procedures necessitated the shedding of blood, the death of innocent animals, on a vast scale. The cost of the first fruits and best animals offered was high. The historian Josephus records over 250,000 lambs slaughtered annually at the *Pesach* (Passover) feast in the 1st Century CE.[58]   The rivers of blood that were shed in monthly and annual ceremonies emphasised the seriousness of falling short of the Creator's standard, and the importance of fulfilling covenant.

---

[57] Deuteronomy 7:9 and 12; 1 Kings 8:23; 2 Chronicles 6:14; Nehemiah 1:5, Psalms 25:10 etc. There is academic debate as to whether covenant is a necessary preconditon for God's *chesed*. As we have found covenant in the beginning, it sets the frame for relationship, and thus for *chesed*, from the beginning.
[58] Josephus, *Wars of the Jews*, Book VI, 9, 3.

Because all of creation or all of humanity or all of Israel cannot be offered to pay the penalty, the temple offerings provided a substitute. They were required because of, not despite, the loving family ties. They stood in the gap before God and were consumed instead of the family being destroyed. The sacrifices maintained the covenant and hence the relationship. That is their purpose.

God cares about that relationship; for example, He stores our tears in a tear bottle (Ps 56:8) and weeps over the fate that Israel brings on herself (Jeremiah 9:1ff) like a parent over a wayward child. The statement that "God (or the Lord) is with us" is repeated seven times in the *Tanach*. Sorrow, suffering and sacrifice can be an expression of love. The Creator too may experience these, such is the depth of His engagement with us. We shall see this in several components of our enquiry.

Covenant encourages or provides the foundation for community. Because it is morally based, moral failure threatens both covenant and the community that derives from it. This enquiry has drawn out the duality between Creator and creation. Family makes for unity but within covenant family, as within our own blood families, there is both strength and fragility, both a dynamic and an underlying and inescapable set of demands.

As a result of covenant, the status of individuals changes; a new identity, a new phase in the development of their character, begins. This happens in marriage and we can also see this happen in Genesis 17 when the names of Abram and Sarai are changed to Abraham and Sarah upon the sealing of the Abrahamic covenant (names being tied to identity in the culture of the time). As with marriage, the new identity can relapse or fail to emerge.

Family gives meaning. Words first take on meaning and life in the context of family relations and families often have distinct or private meanings for everyday words. Similarly, in Biblical Hebrew, meaning is established through covenant. Words such as 'peace' or 'violence' gain their meaning in terms of covenant rather than as statements of aspiration or descriptions of a situation. 'Peace' signifies wholeness of relationship based on fulfilment of covenant, and 'violence' denotes the violation of that. Covenant, and not our own view, is the point of reference.

At the very beginning of the beginning, we find family. In *Torah* scrolls there is no gap between words. The individual words have to be known or deduced from the long string of letters. So, what is the first

recognisable word in the long series of letters that makes up the
Genesis scroll?

Component h: the son

Within *beresheith* (beginning) is *barah* (creation). Within *barah* (creation) is
the first distinguishable word in the Bible: *Bar.*

h)   בר אשית

בר   *bet-reish   Bar*

Bet-reish means 'son'. The word for son is contained within creation
and the opening few letters of the Bible suggest that a father-son
relationship is possible with the Creator.

Just as the absolute distinction between Creator and creation is
immediately established in the Bible, a connection is also established
between the two. It takes the shape of kinship. Psalm 2:7 states: "My
son, today I have begotten Thee." In Exodus 4:22, the Lord refers to
Israel collectively as "my son, my firstborn". Later, Israel collectively
cries out to God as their Father.[59] Praying to "the Lord, our Father",
or simply to "Our Father" is a favourite type of prayer both within
Judaism and Christianity. There is a link, a father-son type of
relationship, which enables the Creator to be addresses as Father. The
presence of the word *bar* here in the beginning emphasises this form of
relationship. It also places it in the context of covenant. The word for
son *(bar)* is encompassed within the word for covenant *(berit)*. This
suggests that the father-son relationship is established fulfilled in
covenant. If we want to understand the one, we need to look at the
other.

Bar is not typically used as the word for son in the *Tanach,* the
word *ben* being more usual. *Bar* is the Aramaic for son, *ben* the Hebrew.
In ten or eleven verses (one is disputed) *bar* is used directly and
explicitly in the sense of son in the Hebrew Bible. Use of the word *bar*
for 'son' is Biblical, but is it valid to consider the Aramaic form?

Discussion of the Hebrew texts of the Bible in Aramaic is normal.
The *Babylonian Talmud* and much of the *Jerusalem Talmud* are written in
Aramaic. Aramaic and Hebrew are closely related languages and some

---

[59] 1 Chronicles 29:10; Isaiah 63:16; Isaiah 64:8.

of the seminal texts for Judaism employ Aramaic and move easily between the two languages. The *Targums* (translations of the Hebrew Bible into Aramaic) use word-plays that occur in Aramaic but not in Hebrew and word-plays between Aramaic and Hebrew to bring out the connotations of Biblical texts. They translate the Hebrew word *ben* into Aramaic as *bar*.

Bar is a familiar word for son in Hebrew. For example, the leader of the great Jewish rebellion against Rome in the early 2nd century was called Bar-Kochba. To this day, the *bar-mitzvah* ceremony marks part of the passage from childhood to adulthood for Jewish children.

Aramaic and Hebrew are closely related and share many words in common. There is debate over their origins, over the nature and extent of borrowings between the two, and over the timing of a move from using Hebrew to Aramaic by the Jewish population of the Holy Land. Aramaic traditions may go back to Abraham who was a native of Aram Naharaim. Indeed, the great rabbinical sage Ramban took the view that Abraham used Aramaic for day-to-day communications.[60] During the period of the Jewish exile in Babylon use of Aramaic appears to have become widespread and by the 1st Century CE Aramaic was well established amongst the Jewish population of the Holy Land.

In the Bible, the Aramaic *bar* is occasionally used for son both before and after the exile to Babylon in the 6th Century BCE. Aramaic has the advantage over Hebrew that the plural form is clearly distinct from the singular whereas in Hebrew usage it is not.[61] Consequently, the Aramaic avoids the occasional uncertainty of Hebrew about whether the singular or plural form of son is intended.

In sum, the Aramaic *bar* for son would be well understood by readers possibly from the earliest Biblical times, and the use of Aramaic in exploring the meaning of Scripture is fully within Judaic traditions. In the case of Genesis 1:1, there is the further prompt that 'son' should be understood as singular not plural.

---

[60] A minority view within Judaism and one ignored or edited out of some commentaries. However, Rabbi Chaim Dov Shaval found this in old manuscripts of Ramban and included it in his edition of Ramban's writings *Sefer HaMitzvot L'HaRambam* published by Mossad Ha-Rav Kook, Jerusalem. Judah Ha Levi (12th Century CE) exposits the same view in *Kuzari*, 2:68.

[61] In Aramaic, the singular *bar* becomes plural *benin*, both adding a suffix and changing a consonant. In Hebrew the singular *ben* becomes plural *banim* with the addition of the letters *yod* and *mem* but in certain usages this plural form is shortened by dropping the *mem*. When written without pointings to the letters - as with the scrolls of the *Tanach* - this is the same as the singular "my son".

With *bar*, as with other components, the *remazim* (hints) lead us to reflect further. As elsewhere in the Bible, there are layers of meaning that require careful consideration. This enquiry is undertaking an exploration, not taking a snapshot.

Beresheith (in the beginning) – the first word of the Bible – contains *barah* (creation), the second word. Hence, the word for son is repeated in the first two words. It is both the first identifiable word and the first repeated word in the Bible. This gives great emphasis to the word as central to understanding how the Creator relates to His creation. In terms of word order, the father-son bond precedes covenant in Gen 1. The word son literally occurs within the word for "in the beginning" and within the word for "creation" but precedes them both. The idea of a son is in the very beginning. The son is first of the first and is found within or leading the act of creation.

Before God first speaks in creative power in Genesis 1:6, there is the son or sons. (We will return later to the question of whether one son or two sons are referred to in the first two words of the Bible.)

As son is the first identifiable word in the Book, God seems eager to speak of this, to introduce the son. This son begins the beginning and stands at the head. We have discovered the head of the house. He stands at the head of the book which is about the relationship between Creator and creation. It follows that the son must be critical to establishing that relationship.[62]

How can relationship between Creator and creation be established through the son figure(s) in terms of covenant? This too is shown in the first few words, as we shall see.

Apart from 'son', there are two other possible meanings of *bar* in the Bible. *Bar* can mean to be pure or clean or that which purifies or cleans, such as lye, potash or alkali used to refine metals. It can also mean a grain of wheat.[63] Both of these meanings bring us back to covenant. The sacrifice in the covenant purifies or cleanses through the fire. Several times in the Bible the fire of the Lord is seen as purifying and refining (Isaiah 48:10, Malachi 3:2, etc.).

The grain offering is one of the sacrifices to be made under the Mosaic covenant. In various verses, grain or bread is compared to God's word.[64] For the second time Genesis 1:1 hints of a connection

---

[62] In Hebrew, the term *ben*, in the sense of "son of", is used to denote a builder of the family name. Indeed, the verb for build is *bana*.

[63] By extension, it is used to mean "field" – as in "animals of the field" – in Daniel 2 and 4.

[64] See Deuteronomy 8:3, Isaiah 55:2, 10, Jeremiah 23:28, Amos 8:11.

to God's word (the first was when we saw that wisdom – God's word – was established in the beginning).

This enquiry has spent some time looking at the word *bet-reish (bar)*. Can much weight be put on two letters that commonly occur together in Hebrew? They are the first two letters of the first two words in the Bible. Therefore, they are worth careful attention, not in isolation but as an element within this enquiry. If what we find yields a coherent whole with the rest of the analysis, then it will be reinforced. It is all part of the same code and *bet-reish* begins that code.

By the same token, if we discount *bar* or any other hint emerging from our examination of the first four words, then we have become selective in that examination and have imposed an external filter on what the words tell us. The enquiry would fail the first of the ten tests listed at the outset: inclusiveness.

Component i: the appointment

There is another figure within *beresheith*. The last three letters in *beresheith* – *shin-yod-tav* – make up the word *sheth*.

i)   בראשית

שית   *shin-yod-tav   Sheth* or *Shet*

Sheth means 'to give', 'to place' or 'to appoint'. It is an irregular root word in Hebrew and in some uses it is spelt without the middle letter, the *yod*, giving us *shin-tav*.[65]

In Genesis 4, Sheth (without the *yod*) is the name of the replacement son given to Adam and Eve for their son Abel, who was murdered by Cain. Eve names him Sheth for she says of him: "God has appointed *(sheth)* to me another seed" (Genesis 4:25).[66] So the word for giving or appointing is also the name of Eve's replacement son, Sheth (or Seth).

In Hebrew thinking, the *yod*, the smallest letter in the Hebrew alphabet, symbolises the metaphysical or life in the world to come. It is

---

[65] In Genesis, the word occurs four times with the *yod* and four times without. In the four subsequent books of the Torah, it occurs eight times without the *yod*, and once with.

[66] The emphasis on the woman's line is unusual but not unique in the *Tanach*.

also the first letter of the ineffable and most holy name of God, YHWH, which is not uttered in Hebrew by those following Rabbinical Judaism. In Hebraic study, variations in spelling of words in the Bible are seen as potentially significant and providing possible clues to hidden meaning in the text. The skipping of the *yod* in Genesis 4 emphasises the earthly nature of the son of Eve called Sheth. Nevertheless, he has great hopes placed upon him by Eve.

The Lord tells the serpent that Eve's seed will crush the serpent's head, in Genesis 3:15. Judaic literature[67], and also Christian, identifies this passage as Messianic. It is the first passage to raise the hope of a Messiah: one anointed by God to sort things out.[68] This is the context for Genesis 4 and the appointment of 'another seed'. Sheth is a God given, replacement son for Eve, and upon him rests Eve's Messianic hope.[69] The first word of Genesis hints at this hope.

In Genesis 4, Eve's son Sheth lacks the *yod*, symbolising the metaphysical, the standing or hope in the life to come. In Genesis 1, the same word appears with the added *yod* to make *shin-yod-tav*. The added *yod* shows that the *sheth* figure of Genesis 1:1 differs from Eve's son Sheth in that the former has the metaphysical aspect that Eve's son lacks. This suggests the fulfilment of Eve's Messianic hope through the metaphysical, through the action of God in connection with the *sheth* of Genesis 1:1. Even before Eve sought a future hope in Genesis 4, it seems the Lord had planned its fulfilment in Genesis 1.

We should not be surprised at this Messianic reference even before the creation of the heavens and the earth in Genesis 1. For example, the *Talmud* states that the name of the Messiah shall endure forever and was ordained before creation.[70] This is on the basis of

---

[67] Notably: by the *Targums* of *Pseudo-Yonathan, Yerushalmi,* and *Neofiti,* which make a play on words with the Aramaic and Hebrew; by *Beresheith Rabbah* 23; and by Rabbi David Kimchi (France, 1160–c1235).

[68] *Beresheith Rabbah* 12:6 sees the Messiah as restoring that which was spoiled by Adam's sin.

[69] This is seen as Messianic by, for example, *Beresheith Rabbah* 23 and *Ruth Rabbah* 8:1. In the first of these, Rabbi Tanhuma (Israel, 5th Century CE) says that "here are we dealing with another seed who is from another place. And who is he? He is the Messiah-King." (*Ruth Rabbah* is an early *midrash*, possibly c3rd–4th Century CE.) In the 19thC, Hirsch, (op.cit., p114) refers to the underlying meaning of the word *sheth* as "foundation" or "support", and to the man Sheth as symbolising a fresh, moral foundation for humanity.

[70] *Talmud, Pesahim* 54a and *Nedarim* 39b. See also *Beresheith Rabbah* 1.4 and 2:4 and 1 Enoch 49:2-3, and 62:7. Footnote 111 below is also relevant.

Psalm 72, which speaks of the reign of a righteous king, and verse 17, which says "May his name endure forever".

The earthly man, Sheth, replaced both Cain and Abel, who were the first two sons of Adam and Eve. Abel took on a priestly role in offering blood sacrifice to the Lord, but was killed by Cain. The murder arose from Cain's anger that the Lord had more regard for Abel's offering than for Cain's. Even before the Abrahamic covenant, blood sacrifice and its association with relationship with the Lord are critical in the Bible's portrayal of human history. Sheth replaces both Abel, the priest figure, and Cain, who was corrupted by sin. All of us, through, Noah, are descended from Sheth in the Biblical account. Indeed, the word *sheth* without the *yod* also means 'six', which is the number of man. Thus, the initial use of the word *sheth* can stand both for all the descendants of Adam and also for the son of Adam who carries the Messianic hope.

In component (d), the head of the house was associated with destitution. Now we come upon duality in the *sheth* figure. He can be said to be heir both to Cain and to Abel. The letters *shin-yod-tav* that make up the word *sheth* can also mean 'thorns' or a 'garment'. In the sense of garment, the word is used twice in the *Tanach* (Psalm 73:6 and Proverbs 7:10). Both times it is used very negatively, suggesting an under-garment of sinfulness and shame. In the sense of thorns, *shin-yod-tav* is repeatedly used in Isaiah to refer to thorns as a symbol of waste and decay: the good ground that has gone bad. (A different word is used for thorns in Genesis 3:18 when God curses the ground.) Hence, the *sheth* figure through these other meanings is associated with shamefulness or waste. Again, there is a duality within *beresheith* concerning a Messianic figure.

The word *sheth* is linked to the word *rosh* (head) within *beresheith*, sharing the letter *shin* in common. This can be seen as emphasising the Divine appointment of the head, perhaps to the Messianic role, or as identifying the head with the *sheth* figure.

Between the *bar* and the *sheth* of components (h) and (i) lies a 'spare' letter *aleph*. We shall return to this later.

Component j: the seat of judgment

As *sheth* means 'to place' or 'to appoint', it is interesting to see how it is placed in the first verse. The word *sheth* is set between the two occurrences of the word *bar* (son) that we previously discussed and thus may be linked to them. Further, the word *sheth* is placed symmetrically between the two occurrences in the first verse of the letters *bet-reish-aleph (barah)*, meaning 'creation' or the act of creation.

בְּרֵא שִׁית בְּרָא

The *sheth* figure is doubly linked with creation and sits exactly between two acts of creation. The text reinforces this by a word that spans *sheth* and the following word, *barah:*

שִׁית בְּ רָא

יתב   *yod-tav-bet   Yetib*

from

ישׁב   *yod-shin-bet   Yashab*

The word *yetib*, a variant of the word *yashab*, means 'to sit' or 'to dwell' and occurs six times in the Bible. Of these, it is used four times in Daniel 7 in the sense of the appointed seat of judgement belonging to the "Ancient of Days".

The appointed figure of *sheth* is appointed to sit or dwell in the central place – literally – amid God's creative acts. There is a hint that this appointment is to a seat of judgement. How or why the *sheth* figure could hold such a central role for all of creation remains to be seen. A greater puzzle is that this figure on the seat of judgement is clothed in shame or decay. Nor does the role of judge sit easily with that of Messiah.

Summary: family

Step three has taken us far from the austere cosmology of creation that Genesis 1:1 presents at first glance and into the warm heart of family: the 'why' of relationship. The Creator's heartbeat is for family and this is transmitted to creation through a son figure and a *sheth* (appointed) figure. These figures carry our hope.

The son figure is the head of the house as he both precedes and is in the beginning, both precedes and is in creation. There is close relationship between the Creator and the son, whom God is eager to introduce to us. 'Son' is the first repeated word in the Bible. The father-son bond is connected to covenant, which is the basis of extending relationship and of bringing us into kinship with the Creator, so as to become family.

A *sheth* figure is similarly central to God's plan for creation. This figure is appointed and represents Eve's Messianic hope in her son Sheth who is also the common ancestor of the human race. The *sheth* figure in Genesis 1:1 contains the metaphysical element that Eve's son, Sheth, lacked. This figure may be the appointed head of creation.

Shadows are found in the beginning. Both the son figure and the *sheth* figure are associated with the blood sacrifice necessary to covenant. As with earthly families that will endure, there is sacrifice and loss in this family. The *sheth* figure may sit in the seat of judgement. This seems antithetical to the idea of building close, family relationship. As with the head discussed in the previous step, there is a possible reversal: the *sheth* figure may be associated with shame or with the good gone bad.

The heartbeat seems troubled. If covenant is the solution to establishing relationship between Creator and creation, and family is the solution to the formal nature of covenant, we are left with tensions and a curious double-edged dynamic. Like ordinary human families, this one looks as if it could be precarious. Like a human family, a strong anchor is needed and we can see hints of this anchor for God's family.

The next step will look into the connections and the seeming fragilities concerned through a fourth and final way of dividing up the first word in Genesis. Step four will reveal more of the dynamics that the Creator has set in train and concludes our discussion of the Bible's first word, a word that leaves us with much to digest.

So far, the discussion has bred complexity. Each component adds more points to digest. But this is not just an ever growing accumulation of points; one can see linkages and areas where the pieces look as if they will fit together. As we press forward, some aspects of this complexity will increase, but the harmonies will become stronger also. Later steps will begin to resolve the complexity into a single clear picture and rhythm.

Step Four: Broken Connections

The first word; third deliberation. A final way of dividing the first word, which shows the 'what' of relationship. Giving and receiving. Forging close relationship between Creator and creation.

W e have found His family to which we can belong, but the heartbeat seems troubled. By going deeper, can we grasp what ails this family – our family – and discover the cure? Pieces of the puzzle have been found, but so far the puzzle becomes greater.

At the gateway to the Bible, we are confronted with a mystery. Because of its location, the mystery must be fundamental to understanding creation and to understanding the Creator. The opening verse of Genesis both describes the first act of creation and presents a Creator who remains closely engaged. He is engaged in a particular way, though we still have much to fathom about this way and its problematic consequences. That engagement seems to bring problems, demands and uncertainties. Understanding how these are resolved will equip us to comprehend all that follows in the Bible.

The previous steps divided up the opening word, *beresheith*, and looked at its components in three different ways:

- into *beth* (house, temple) plus *rosh* (head / destitution)

- into *berit* (covenant) plus *esh* (flame / foundation)

- into *bar* (son / purity / grain of wheat) plus *sheth* (to appoint / Eve's son, Sheth) plus a 'spare' *aleph*.

The first word is not yet exhausted. This step explores a further way of dividing it into separate components and illustrates how the four different ways of cutting *beresheith* can be drawn together to build a single, unified story.

Step four provides fresh components to consider from within *beresheith*. These yield new clues as to how relationship is forged between Creator and creation. This step will conclude our examination of the first word in the Bible.

Component k: the tree

Let us return to the remarkable word *beresheith*. Again, set aside its third letter, *aleph*, to which we will return. The first, second and fourth letters give us *bet-reish-shin*. This word, with or without an additional silent letter *vav*, has the same meaning and pronunciation.

k)   בר א שׁ ית

בר שׁ *bet-reish-shin* or ברושׁ *bet-reish-vav-shin* *Berosh*

Berosh means a 'tree', a type of conifer.[71] Step six, which looks at the word *Elohim*, yields a second and separate reference to a tree within the opening words of Genesis. But here, in the middle of *Beresheith*, sits a common type of conifer tree.

In Genesis 1:1, the letter *yod* follows *berosh*. With its inclusion at the end of *berosh*, the word becomes 'my tree', that is God's tree. Elsewhere in the *Tanach*, the word *berosh* is mentioned along with other types of tree. What has the Lord to do with this type of tree in particular; in what sense is it His?

Two passages give us a hint. In Isaiah 55:13 the *berosh* tree is described as coming up instead of the thornbush as "a memorial to the Lord, for an everlasting sign which will not be cut off." It seems the *berosh* is an eternal sign. We will return to this sign later.

At the conclusion of Hosea, in Hosea 14:8/9, the Lord says "I am like a green cypress *(berosh)*; from Me comes your fruit." Unexpectedly,

---

[71] Which type is subject to debate and the word is variously translated as a cypress, fir or juniper tree. The root word is *bet-reish-shin*. In the Bible it is written with the letter *vav* inserted between the *reish* and the *shin*, except at 2 Kings 19:23 where the plural form *beroshim* appears to be used as a simile for the temple.

the Lord explicitly likens Himself to this humble kind of tree. The statement is all the more unexpected since conifers are not fruit trees; they do not yield fruit for human consumption. However, their cones can be burnt in the fire. Their fruit is for the fire, perhaps the *esh* that we came across at component (g).

The Lord likens Himself to a green *(raanan)* tree in Hosea 14:8/9. Eleven times *raanan* is combined with the more general term for tree *(ets)* and always refers to a place of false worship. It seems trees are dangerous places. The significance of the *berosh* tree located here in the beginning needs to be clearly identified, so that we do not err into a place of false worship. We must be careful in our deliberations not to jump to conclusions. Hence the need for the exhaustive process of analysing each word that is adopted for this enquiry.

Berosh can occur with or without the letter *vav*. Here, within the first word of the Bible, it is spelt without the *vav*. In Hebrew thought, the letter *vav* symbolises completion. Elsewhere in the Bible, the omission of this letter from the normal spelling of a word is held to mark incompletion. Its omission here could refer to something that is incomplete or only partially complete.

In *beresheit* the letter *aleph* occurs in the place of the omitted letter *vav*. It is the letter that was skipped in the middle of 'my tree':

בר **א** שׁי

Standing on its own, *aleph* means the number 'one', or 'unity'. Symbolically, in Hebraic thought, the *aleph* stands for the head or father of the whole house, primarily God Himself or Adam. Judaic writers have commented on the dichotomy of *aleph* standing both for God and for Adam, who is the first or representative man.[72] In Hebrew thought the linkage between the two can be seen in the written form of the *aleph*. With one vertical stroke higher than the other and the diagonal connecting them, this represents a ladder between man and God. The formation of the letter *aleph* stands for the connection between God and man. In Genesis 1:1 the *aleph* could indicate the presence of God, or an Adam figure, or a connection between them amid the tree. However, this connection is incomplete because of the omission of the *vav* which stands for completion.

---

[72] In Hebrew, the word *adam* (or more precisely *ha adam,* 'the adam') is used as the term for all of Israel, for humanity generally and for our origin in Adam.

Earlier, we found the term for fire within the word for covenant. Now we find the letter *aleph* within the word for 'my tree' and that same fire has taken hold of the tree through the *aleph*.

בר א שׁי   *Eshy*   My fire

One could say that the fire has been ignited by the introduction of the *aleph* into the word *berosh*. Because of the *aleph*, the sacrificial fire of covenant burns God's tree or perhaps burns its fruit.

In the last step, the letter *aleph* stood alone between *bar* (the word for son) and *sheth* (the word for 'to appoint' or for Eve's son Sheth). Again the letter stands by itself. We shall keep finding it standing on its own, and we shall discuss the import of this further at step nine.

The middle three letters of *beroshi* ('my tree') constitute the word for head that was noted in component (d). Just as the fire has taken hold of the tree, the head in some sense is in the tree.

ברא וׁ י

Contained within covenant is a tree, and within that tree are the *aleph* and the head and the fire that the *aleph* has lit. We are given a set of inter-linked images, nested within each other. The *aleph* is the symbol for the link between God and man; the head is the head of the house of all creation; the fire is the covenant fire. They are linked together through the tree. What are they doing there? And the tree is contained within covenant. What is it doing there?

To return to Hosea 14:8/9, this verse provides a possible connection. As we have said, the verse reads "I am like a luxuriant cypress *(berosh)*; from Me comes your fruit." The word "like" in this translation comes from the Hebrew letter *bet* used as a prefix. In the *Tanach* the letter *bet* is it more typically is used in the sense of 'in' or 'at'. Genesis 1:1 begins with the letter *bet* used to mean 'in'. This meaning could also be implied at Hosea 14:8/9: "I am (with)in a luxuriant cypress *(berosh)*; from Me comes your fruit." As we have seen, the head and the *aleph* are within the tree. Perhaps symbolically the head or the *aleph* yield fruit (with)in the tree. The meaning, however, remains obscure.

We have spent some time on the word *berosh* in order to follow up every connection it suggests. The result has been rather dizzying but we must see if the pieces fit with the broader picture emerging. To do less would be to ignore or gloss over the text. By relentlessly pursuing every clue of every component we avoid being selective and test our method to the limit. Can all these little clues and hints fit together; do the dots connect up ?

Component I: the gift

Within the tree *berosh*, there is a further combination. The letter *aleph* separates the letters *bet-reish* (*bar*, meaning "son") from the letters *shin-yod* within the word 'my tree'. Thus:

I)   בר א ש י

ש י   *shin-yod   Shay*

The two letters *shin* and *yod* together mean 'gift' *(shay)*. This is always used in the sense of a tribute or gift of homage the three times it appears in the *Tanach* (Psalm 68:29, Psalm 76:11, Isaiah 18:7). In the context of Genesis 1:1, this must be a gift offered from creation back to the Creator.

This tribute cannot refer to the temple offerings that fulfilled the Mosaic covenant. These were, of course, not in the beginning and such actions came to an end with the destruction of the Jerusalem temple in 70 CE. Consequently, that method of renewing covenant ended. The gift of tribute in Genesis 1:1 is likely to refer to something enduring. Indeed, the offerings in the Jerusalem temple may in some sense refer to or symbolise this enduring gift, or be a partial earthly fulfilment of it. But, what is the gift of homage hidden within 'my tree'?

The gift is joined by the *aleph* to the son figure *(bar)* in the context of 'my tree'. Taken together, the components of son and of gift of homage constitute the word 'my tree', with the *aleph* being 'spare'. This set of components is revealed or fulfilled in the tree or the tree is revealed or fulfilled through this set of components. In some sense the tree yields a gift of homage. We must pursue our enquiry further to obtain a clear idea of what the gift and its implications are and to see whether we can explain the *aleph* being left over.

If we remove the final *yod*, which stands for the first person possessive 'my', then we have 'the tree' rather than 'my tree'. With the *yod* removed, the letter *aleph* separates the word for son not from the word for gift but from the letter *shin*.

בר א ש   *bet-reish aleph shin*

It is a fragment, but consider the *shin* in terms of what else we have found. *Shin* as a letter on its own is understood in Hebrew thought to represent both divine power and also corruption or evil. This is a startling juxtaposition of ideas but reflects the nature of sacrifice within covenant: an unblemished victim stands in for a party to the covenant and takes on their faults and failings in that covenant. Hence, in the context of the tree, the son is connected through the *aleph* to the sign of both divine power and of corruption, just as previously we saw the word *sheth* connected both to priestly sacrifice and to corruption. [73]

Earlier we found that *rosh*, the word for head, can also mean destitution and that the *sheth* figure is associated both with judgement and with shame. There are a range of dualities here and consequent uncertainty as to whether it is divine power or corruption that is seen. Similarly, if we do not see the tree as 'my tree' – that is 'His tree' – then we do not know whose tree it is. Consequently, the gift of tribute may not be seen. Instead there is uncertainty as to whether it is divine power or corruption that is displayed in the context of the tree.

Through a strange set of hints, the text invites the reader to resolve the puzzle but beware of the dualities and uncertainties.

Component m: brokenness, conclusion

Following the word for 'my tree' is the last letter of the word *beresheith*, the letter *tav* on its own. The *tav* points us forward to the next word, *barah*, discussed in the following chapter. If we combine *tav*, the last letter of *beresheith*, with the first two letters of *barah*, we obtain *tebar*, a form of *shebar* meaning to be 'fragile' or 'broken'.

m)   ת בר א

---

[73] In Deuteronomy 21:23, it is said "anyone who is hung on a tree is under God's curse". However, the word used there for tree is *ets*, not *berosh*.

תבר or שבר *Tebar* or *Shebar*

In the form *tebar*, the word only occurs once in the Bible in Daniel 2:42. The name of the mountain Tabor – with an additional *vav* – derives from it and occurs ten times. [74] In the more familiar form *shebar*, the word usually describes the consequences of judgement.

Earlier in component (j) we saw that the seat of judgement of the *sheth* figure spanned the gap between the first and second words of Genesis. Now we find that brokenness resulting from judgement similarly spans that gap. The *sheth* figure is associated both with judgement and with the brokenness resulting from judgement.

The brokenness of component (m) also links to the word preceding it, the gift of component (l).

שׂי תבר

This combination suggests a gift being broken in sacrifice as a consequence of judgement. This brokenness may also be connected to the remaining letter of the second word, a 'spare' *aleph*, one of a number of 'spare' *alephs* to which we shall turn later.

Both the first and second words of Genesis contain the word *barah* (creation). As we shall see at the next step, the gap between them corresponds to the period between the first and second creation. Components (j) and (m) bridge that gap and hint at what lies between. They hint that this is when the breaking of a sacrificial gift in judgement occurs.

The *tav* as the concluding letter of *beresheith* can be looked at on its own. It was also left over when we looked at 'His tree" in component (k). The *tav* is the last letter of the Hebrew alphabet and in Hebraic thought stands for the end and the conclusion. The tree and what is associated with it lead to the end and conclusion. The end is already in the beginning. If so, then it flows from the tree and the components that we found within the tree.

---

[74] Mount Tabor can be identified as the mountain that Israel is called to offer righteous sacrifices upon in Deuteronomy 33:18/19. According to the *Yalkut Shimoni* on that passage, it was the location for the temple if no specific instruction had been given. (The *Yalkut Shimoni* is a compilation of commentaries, possibly from the 13thC CE.) Jeremiah 46:18 compares the "one who is to come" – probably the Messiah – to Tabor and to Carmel (*carmel* means literally 'a fruitful field' or 'vineyard').

This enquiry looks at individual letters when examination of the structure and patterns within the first verse draws attention to them. The *tav* is the third individual Hebrew letter we have singled out for attention. The connotation of individual letters – fragments – on their own can be given little weight in examining the verse but as part of a message or code they can be revealing. Here the *tav* connects a (or the) conclusion with the tree and hints that this conclusion is in turn connected to brokenness and to the consequences of judgement.

Summary: the first word

The survey of the first word in the Bible, *beresheith*, is complete. In Hebraic practice, the first word of the book provides the title of the book, and so it is with the five books of the *Torah*. Hence, all the details we have unpacked from within the word *beresheith* also provide a statement as to the contents of the first book of the Bible, *Beresheith*.

Step four has been our third and final deliberation upon the opening word of the Bible, a word that has been 'cut' in four different ways in the process of this enquiry. The enquiry has examined every component emerging from these different cuts in order to leave nothing unconsidered and to extract the maximum possible information. The components we have found provide the connections that build up the story hidden within the opening word.

This step has shown us a series of connections: perhaps the 'what' or fabric of relationship. But the connections seem to be broken, the fabric torn.

We have found 'my tree', a tree where completion is lacking. The *aleph*, the sign for the link between God and man, is trapped there and can be linked both to divine power and to corruption. It separates – or connects – the letters that stand for son from the letters that stand for a gift of homage paid to God. Similarly, the word meaning 'head' is found within the tree. The tree is ignited by fire stemming from the *aleph*, and maybe its fruit is burnt. The tree and the components it contains lead to the consequences of judgement, where a gift is broken, and to a conclusion. There is giving and there is receiving, but the nature and precise context of the gift remain a puzzle.

As with the previous deliberations, we find dualities and uncertainties. The tree can be a place of false worship, of going astray. The fruit of the tree may be fit only for burning. Divine power can become enmeshed with corruption.

The complex layering of words or letters within words provides a rich, if puzzling, dynamic. Are we going too far in following such routes? We are looking at what is there in the Hebrew text and we remain within the strict rules stated at the outset. We are listening to what the text tells us and unpacking its meaning. Nothing in the Hebrew has been changed and every clue is pursued. It remains to be seen if the pieces will fit together and to test the results.

Some of our findings are fragments: single letters or pairs of letters. In isolation, little weight can be attached to their possible meanings or references. However, in combination with our other findings, these fragments can help build a picture. The fragments as such are neither accepted nor rejected. Instead, they are treated as possible pieces of a greater whole.

Much is hidden "in the beginning". The unique use of the word *beresheith* in Scripture, the difficulty in grasping its precise meaning, and its place at the head of Scripture and as the title of the opening book to the *Torah*, all invite attention. One commentator describes *beresheith* as having a "fractal structure" (that is, a complex pattern reproduced at every level) that foreshadows the structure of the *Torah*.[75] We have examined thirteen different components: words that can be found within the first word with their various distinct meanings, as well as the symbolism of four Hebrew letters that stand on their own or modify one or more of those words.[76]

We have found a God who cares. As Psalm 23 puts it: "The Lord is my shepherd, I shall not want." However, we are left with tensions and contradictions. Close relationship is desired but the shedding of blood is required by covenant. How is this to be without the Jerusalem temple? Close relationship suggests informality and dynamism, yet covenant is fixed and formal in nature. We have responsibilities toward the Creator but it is difficult to meet them. If covenant sacrifice is the solution to the great divide between Creator and creation, it produces its own problems.

---

[75] Ellis, Richard S (1997) "The Book of Leviticus and the Fractal Geometry of Torah," *Conservative Judaism*, 50.1, 27–34.

[76] In *Tikunei Zohar,* a commentary on the book of Genesis, each of its 70 sections starts with a different interpretation of the word *beresheith*. This is primarily by using pairs of letters generated from the word both directly and by a transformational process. Using the numerical values of words, the Vilna Gaon claimed that the first word *beresheith* contains allusions to all 613 commands of the Mosaic Law. As our approach is much stricter, we do not face such overwhelming quantity of allusion!

We glimpse a Creator intimately involved with His creation. The components looked at in *beresheith* show us how God founds His family. He reaches out across the divide. There is giving and receiving but there is uncertainty as to the nature of the transaction. Dualities become apparent and confront us.

The Hebrew word for "in the beginning", with its complexity and the different ways its component parts can be unpacked, is itself only the beginning. Its patterns and puzzles, with their half glimpsed resolutions, encourage us to look further and press on with our voyage of discovery. *Beresheith* has revealed both the gulf between Creator and creation, and the outline of a solution. It has shown a dynamic that is rooted in the beginning and that is still underway, that is complete but not yet completed.

Far from being some grand, vague statement, Genesis 1:1 contains many specifics: the Creator seeks relationship and in a specific way; the head of the house has particular characteristics associated with him; and so forth. The Creator is not sending us an anodyne greeting card with His opening words. But is there a key to unlock what lies before us?

Step Five: The Arrow

The second word. The nature of God's continuing creative engagement with His creation. His plan for history.

P salm 19 states that "The heavens declare the glory of God". The Psalm goes on to tell us that the word of God restores the soul, makes the simple wise, rejoices the heart, enlightens the eyes and is sweeter than honey. Sadly, this is not a common experience, even for those who earnestly study it. Yet, there can be a real hunger to know the Creator. This enquiry aims to encourage the reader to pursue God, and all the more as we discover how He pursues us and at what cost.

A rhythm is emerging, the outlines of a key. The message of Genesis 1:1 goes beyond what can be seen on the surface and its components form a discernible architecture. The message is encoded, but it is not unbreakable. Our task is to uncover the code that is folded into the opening statement about creation and to unfold it as carefully as possible. The declaration of the Bible's first verse concerns creation and the glory of God revealed in creation. But does it give understanding of the Creator's intent for His creation and for us and can we grasp such a matter?

With step five we turn to the second word, a word we have already come across within the first word: creation. The Bible proceeds to its second word and already it repeats itself. Is this mere repetition or something more?

Component n: creation for the second time

The second word in the Bible is *barah*, meaning 'creation'.

n)   בָּרָא   *bet-reish-aleph   Barah*

Barah was contained in the first word and discussed under
component (b). The repetition suggests the need to look closely at
what is happening with this word *barah*. It highlights both the act of
creation and the figure of the son, who is contained within *barah* when
the final letter *aleph* is removed. Standing at the head of the whole
Bible gives huge emphasis to both the act of creation and to the word
for son and ties them firmly together. They set the rhythm for the
heartbeat.

In the first chapter of Genesis, on the sixth day of creation and
after He has created humanity and given Adam instructions, God looks
and sees all that He had made and "behold, it was very good". Then,
on the seventh day, He rests.

Is this the end of God's involvement with His creation, the end of
His role in our story? No: we know from the rest of the book that He
remains very involved. Is it the end of God's creative acts? No:
although some translations muddy this, the root term *barah* for creation
or the act of creating is only used infrequently after the creation
account in Genesis of God's activity. But it is so used. Even the form
of the first two Hebrew words suggests something ongoing in the
Creator's act of creation; it is not only "in the beginning".

The repetition of the word *barah* in the first verse of the Bible
points to these subsequent creative acts by the Creator. It
demonstrates that God has not retired from His creation. Having set
the mechanisms of the created world in motion, his activity does not
end. In looking at the opening statement of the Bible, we are not, so to
speak, jammed up in the initial burst of creation. The second *barah*
invites a broader perspective in considering the beginning.

The question of the role of the Creator is not restricted to origins
– how did things start – or of working through set processes. Like the
parent who remains engaged with their children, the question is one of
relationship <u>now</u>. And as with the parent who remains engaged, this
makes the matter far more pressing, indeed far more hazardous. A set
order of creation does not continue operating within given rules, left to
run – or run down – by its Creator. Nor does He simply control
creation or suffuse it, nor is He identical with it or in some sense

subordinate to it or its rules. The Creator is not safely off the scene, nor is He part of the scenery.

Something else is going on here, which does not correspond with those human philosophies – whether Eastern or Western, modern or ancient – that derogate the role of the Creator. The repetition of the word *barah* in the first words of Genesis helps us grasp what this 'something else' is. It shows that there is a history to the Creator's engagement with creation and thus a history to creation written in terms of that engagement. The Creator cannot be restricted to being only the First Cause of creation. If there are subsequent applications of His creative power, then to understand creation we have to understand the nature of that ongoing engagement.

The word *barah* is repeated in Genesis 1:1 before the heavens and the earth are mentioned at all. This gives primacy to the act(s) of creation and to the time dimension, as against the physical dimensions: that which is created. To understand the latter we must first look to the former. Only looking at the created, physical world is insufficient to gain understanding of creation.

Barah is used in terms of the Creator action in seven distinct ways. In creation week – the first seven days described in Genesis 1 – it is used:

- of the heavens and the earth, their contents and the forces of the cosmos

- of animate life

- of human beings.

With the completion of the physical creation, God moves to a different kind of creation which involves His interaction with humanity and our education and development. Subsequent to Genesis 1, *barah* is used of:

- Israel

- a new people

- righteousness

- a new heavens and a new earth, including a new Jerusalem.

Let us look briefly at these last four kinds of creation.

First, *barah* is used of the creation of God's chosen people – Jacob, Israel – in Isaiah 43:1 and 15 and Isaiah 65:18. The Bible refers to God's creative miracles in respect of Israel at Exodus 34:10, Isaiah 4:5

and 41:20 and to a negative miracle (that is a punishment) at Numbers 16:30. In any event, God is involved in His creative power with Israel, His chosen people.

Second, *barah* is used of "a people yet to be created who may praise the Lord" (Psalm 102:18/19) and of "everyone who is called by My Name" in Isaiah 43:7. Whether these references are to a new or renewed Israel or to a wider group is a matter for debate. The Psalm may suggest a distinction between Israel (already created and benefiting from God's ongoing creative miracles) and the people who, at the time of writing, had yet to be created. God is involved, or in future will be involved, in His creative power with those who praise Him and those who are called by His name. Possibly, this looks beyond Israel.

Third, *barah* is used of righteousness, in Psalm 51:10 when the Psalmist cries out "Create in me a clean heart, O God", in Isaiah 45:8 when the Lord says He has created salvation and righteousness and in Isaiah 57:19 when the Lord creates the praise of the lips. God responds in His creative power to those who cry out to Him for righteousness.

Fourth, *barah* is used of the new or renewed creation at Isaiah 65:17 and 65:18. Indeed, the two appearances of the word *barah* within the first two words of Genesis – *Beresheith barah* – give an inkling of this new creation. As with the need for a new beginning, there will be need for a new heaven and a new earth. The reason why is also hinted at in Genesis 1.

We see the Lord's intense ongoing creative engagement with humanity, but not all of humanity. The Creator's selective use of His creative power is, so to speak, His arrow through time, His plan. The Creator and His creation are separate and the Creator now focuses His creative power from the general to the specific. The initial act of creation was purposeful and the subsequent focus must be also. In that case, the nature of His creative involvement, shown by the later uses of the word *barah*, indicates His plan for creation. What's it all about? The Bible's first verse both describes the initial creation and hints at the plan and purpose of it all. The repetition of the word *barah* tells us that there is more and gives us an arrow to follow.

As discussed in step one, *barah* means creation from nothing. This is distinct from making or forming something from something else. In the Bible, God mostly makes and rarely creates. We make things, and in Genesis 1 God made – *asah* – the expanse, made the two great lights, and made the stars in the creation account. That is to say, He formed them from pre-existing material. In terms of the appearance of human beings on the scene, both the words for make and for create are deployed in the Genesis account. God uses pre-existing material and then injects something new to create human life on the sixth day. Whatever that something new is, it could not be shaped or formed from pre-existing material. It needs the creative power of God.

The distinction between God's acts of creation and acts of making tells us how significant and remarkable each such creative act is. These acts include the creation of Israel and the creation of a clean heart and of praise in those who seek Him. These acts tell us how involved God is with us. It is startling to think that the creation of a clean heart in a human being is a greater act of God than the making of the stars in the universe. God shows His concern for us as the pinnacle of creation.

The Creator has a purpose for His creation and He acts purposefully in pursuit of that. There is a plan and in that plan lies our fulfilment and the fulfilment of all creation. For example, when Psalm 96 declares "Sing to the Lord a new song; sing to the Lord, all the earth" and "Let the heavens be glad and the earth rejoice" (verses 1 and 11), the picture is of all creation rejoicing before the Lord, led by us.

A Divine plan begins to be revealed, but its implications are disturbing. If God is still actively involved with His creation, then the problem of the pain and confusion of the world becomes more pressing. Can He not put it right? Where is God's creative power to be seen and why is He selective in its use? And how does this interact with our role?

After verses 1 and 2, the account in Genesis 1 repeatedly uses the composition that God says "let there be" and then "it was so". The involvement of God with His creation entails the Creator speaking and a response to that: His creation listens and responds obediently. There is a moral character to the action, even before the creation of humanity. With humanity this is carried further and with Israel and the giving of the His Law to Israel further still. His word is given and we can choose obedience to it, or not. The focus of God's creative power on Israel directly continues the creation saga and the moral framework of Genesis 1. Stories of origin in other cultures set the moral framework for subsequent events. The distinctive of Genesis is that this framework is laid out across the fault-line of the absolute distinction between the all-powerful Creator and His creation.

Concomitant to God's engagement with His creation is our obedience: that is, we have the choice to align and engage with His purpose and engage with Him, or not. It follows that there is the possibility for disobedience. Our potential can be fulfilled, or not.

God's creative power can be experienced as destruction where there is disobedience, as with Numbers 16:30 or as with the great day of the Lord, a day of destruction and terror which ends the current age. Engagement with the Creator is both necessary and, apparently, dangerous. How can we be equipped for such a mission?

We are not automatically obedient and we can tend to move away from alignment with His plan and purpose. In this our potential is squandered. The message that is emerging is that if we move away, there are consequences but the Creator provides a way for us to move back. The need is great: for God to create a clean heart in a person implies that there is a deep lack on the side of humanity; we are unable to achieve a clean heart ourselves. Something new has to be created by God from nothing and added to us, otherwise 'making' rather than 'creating' would be involved.

In the dynamic between the person who seeks God and He who is sought, each has freedom and each is bound to the other through their mutual concern. The bond is by means of covenant where they become family. This lies at the heart of *barah*. The Creator can limit and focus His actions and choose to be bound by them, through entering into covenant relationship.

The repetition of *barah* in Genesis 1:1 raises the question of whether, in some sense, there are two creations or acts of creation. We have seen that the Creator continues to be involved in creative power with His creation. But is this pointing toward an end point, a second general act of creation? In its first appearance, the word for creation is followed by the word *sheth*, which refers to the appointment of the earthly man, Sheth (component (i) above). In its second appearance, *barah* is followed by the word *Elohim* which refers to God. The first creation that is hinted at here through the first appearance of *barah* is primarily earthly in focus. In the second creation, hinted at by the second appearance of *barah*, the Divine is revealed directly.

The word *bar*, son, is contained within each appearance of *barah*. The son figure (or figures) is (or are) connected to both acts of creation and must be critical to them. Any solution to the entry code must explain this double connection.

If there are two creations, this indicates a crisis or insufficiency in the first, a need to put matters right. The putting right is the reason for sacrifice, as shown earlier. In that case, the sacrifice found embedded in the beginning leads from the first creation – within which matters need to be put right – into the second creation. Between these two creations must occur the 'putting right'.

Components (j) and (m) indicated the nature of this 'putting right'. These two words that link the first and second appearances of *barah* in Genesis 1:1:

- *yetib* or *yeshib* meaning to sit in judgement and referring to the *sheth* figure

- *tebar* or *shebar* meaning brokenness in judgement.

The *sheth* figure sits exactly between the two appearances of *barah* and thus is central to God's action between the first and second creation. In this action, a judgement that breaks is involved. Confirming this, we have also seen that the gap between the first and second words in Genesis is associated with a gift being broken in sacrifice.

Embedded in the construction of Genesis 1:1 is a timeline within which a story unfolds. The events subsequent to – consequent upon – the first creation are outlined: a gift of homage is broken in sacrifice as a consequence of judgement involving the *sheth* figure. The hints of a partial completion found previously also lead us here. The completion of the first creation is not a full completion. That awaits the second creation.

This plan is not limited to a local arrangement for *homo sapiens* on planet earth and neighbourhood. Genesis 1:1 is the story of all creation and the plan is for all creation – the heavens and the earth – with us at the centre.

We have seen that the first and second words are connected by words that can be read across between them. To conclude the discussion of the second word, we should check whether there are any connecting words that can be deduced to link it with the following word. *Barah* ends with the letter *aleph* and the next word *Elohim* begins with the same letter. Consequently, unlike the ending of *beresheith* and the beginning of *barah*, there are no words that can be deduced from the text that span the two.

Summary: the arrow

Genesis 1:1 tells us the basis of the Creator's ongoing involvement with His creation through the repetition of the word *barah* and the different focii of its two appearances. This leaves us to grapple with the nature of God's role in history and the time puzzle of two creations.

The two *barahs* show us a God who is not outside history, but creatively engaged with us. From the span of all creation, the focus narrows. Between the first and second creation, the Creator continues His involvement in creative power with what He has created, but this is selective. This dynamic leaves space for us to determine our own direction, whether that is away from or toward Him.

To understand the dynamic between Creator and creation, we need this book – the Bible – as a counterpoint to prevailing worldviews. The repetition of the word *barah* propels us forward to ask the nature of the Creator's actions and plan for us, to ask how we can fulfil our part as the pinnacle of creation. This is to follow the trajectory of the arrow shot forth from the opening words.

Between the great event of the first creation and the great event of the second creation, something happens that is closely related to both. The two creations are not mere book-ends to the meaty reading that lies in between. Nor is there empty space between them. Between the two creations, the Creator interacts with His creation. There is direction and purpose to His engagement and there is choice for us in how we join with Him. There is a storyline and we contribute to the story.

The flight path of the arrow is not yet clear. One of the ten tests listed at the outset for the results from this enquiry was coherence and that "the story should be complete and without loose ends." Therefore, as this enquiry proceeds, we should expect that it will reveal more about God's history and plan for creation. The results should provide coherence and completion to that history.

The next step considers the Divine and gives an inkling of His perspective on the storyline within the opening words.

Step Six: The Creator's Heartbreak

The third word by which the Creator is made known. The 'who' of
the relationship in terms of the role He plays. The cost of His
engagement.

A t last the Creator puts in an appearance with the third word.
Examining the first two words has helped us to understand
something of the act of creation and of the Creator in relation to His
creation. The third word speaks directly of Him: it is where God
reveals Himself. In this step, we consider the Creator's perspective on
His relationship with His creation. We find that He is hurting and that:
"Indeed, You are a God who conceals Himself, the God of Israel is the
Saviour". (Isaiah 45:15) He hides so that we will seek Him.

Our discussion of the previous two words helps focus and inform
consideration of the third word. Parallels emerge.

Component o: *Elohim*

The third word in the opening phrase is *elohim:*

o)   בראשית ברא אלהים את

אלהים *Elohim*   אל *El*

Elohim is one of the names of God and the first one revealed in the Bible. In Judaic thought, *Elohim* (from *el* meaning 'strong') is usually considered to speak of the God of judgement.[77] *Elohim* begins with the letter *aleph*, which itself can stand for God or the connection between Him and humanity.

The word is in the plural, employing a standard form for the plural by adding *yod-mem* to the end of the word *Eloha* ('lord'). Both *Eloha* and *El* are also used as terms for God in the *Tanach* but *Elohim* is the term used most frequently. Genesis 1:1 is both the first appearance of the name of God used most frequently in the Bible and the first appearance of the plural form in the Bible. The associated verb for the act of creation is in the singular, as generally occurs in the *Tanach* when the term *Elohim* is used to refer to God. It is widely accepted that the plural *Elohim* is an honorific title – the royal 'we' – although the Hebrew kings do not use this style of address in the Bible.

First appearances in the Bible are thought to hold special significance. How odd if the double first of *Elohim* (of naming the Creator and of a plural form in the *Tanach*) turns out to be a blind alley. We must, therefore, consider the possibility that this first plural in the Bible is telling us something. In any event, our method requires that we investigate each hint that we come across.

The Hebrew language allows a complex plurality to be contained within a unity. Thus, the Hebrew word *echad* is used to refer both to the concept of 'one' and of a complex unity where a plural is treated as a unified whole. For example, the unity *(echad)* that is Israel or the unity that is the Mosaic Law both contain a complex plurality: Israel consists of more than one tribe, the Law consists of more than one rule. Yet, they are both *echad*.

Battle lines have developed between Judaic and Christian theologians over the Christian concept of God as a trinity or tri-une God, as against strict monotheistic Judaism. Such a sharp divide scarcely reflects usage in Biblical times and seems to be a later construct, reflecting the bitter division that grew up.[78] The book of Proverbs states that wisdom – or the word of God – was there at the beginning of creation. Based on that and other references, some Judaic writers and translators refer to wisdom and the word or the spirit of God as if they were distinct elements within a unified God-head and

---

[77] This thought appears to originate from the *Sifre Devarim* 27 (1st-2ndC CE).

[78] See Nassi, Tzvi (1970) *The Great Mystery,* Yanetz, Jerusalem.

the idea of a tri-unity or plurality within the one God is to be found in various Judaic sources.[79]

The original concern within Judaism was to distinguish between the one universal, almighty and unique Creator God and the many local Gods of the pagans, rather than whether more than one element could be spoken of in some sense within that one, supreme Deity. Thus, the *Shma*, the central declaration of Judaism: "Hear *(shma)*, O Israel, the Lord thy God, the Lord is one *(echad)*." (Deuteronomy 6:4). In his commentary on the *Shma*, Rashi sees God as becoming *echad* when He is accepted as the God of all. In the mid 1stC CE the Jewish apostle of Christ, Paul or Shaul, a self-declared Pharisee, refers insistently to the *echad* of the *Shma*, stating that "God is only one".[80] In the context of 1st Century CE Judaism, finding more than one element within the one God, as Paul / Shaul did, was not a flagrant contradiction.[81]

We should not to be distracted by later theological divisions from seeing the hint in the third word of Genesis that the one universal Creator God who acts in unity may contain more than one aspect or element within that unified Godhead. Of course, the nature of that unity is hard for us to comprehend. In terms of this enquiry, the focus narrows to how this hint within the word *Elohim* fits with, and is supported by, hints from the other components to build the entry code: what is God telling us in the beginning?

---

[79] See the use of the *Mimra,* meaning "the word of God", in the *Targums* of *Pseudo-Yonathan, Nefiti,* and *Onkelos,* e.g. "Abraham believed in the Lord's *Mimra* and it was credited to him as righteousness" (Genesis 15:6) or in Deuteronomy 28 the substitution of the *"Mimra* of the Lord" for many references to "the Lord", including where the Lord takes various actions. In terms of later writings, the *Zohar,* a magical form of Judaism, refers to three aspects of God being united in one (Amsterdam edition *Zohar,* II, 43a; III, 65 and III, 288). (The *Zohar* is traditionally said to have originated in the 2nd Century CE with Shimeon Ben Yohai.) The poet of the liturgy, Eliezar Kalir (6th Century CE or earlier), in the *Book of Creation* and Rabbi Menachem of Recananti (Italy 1223–1290) in *Commentary on the Pentateuch* write of the tri-une nature of the Divine. Hirsch refers to a plurality subsumed within a unity (Hirsch, op.cit., p649).

[80] Galatians 3:20. Similarly: "there is no God but one ... there is but one God, the Father, from whom are all things, and we exist for Him." (1 Corinthians 8:4–6) Paul goes on to say "and one Lord, Jesus Christ, by whom are all things and we exist through Him.". Of course, the latter assertion would have caused disagreement. The contemporary Anglican theologian N T Wright has drawn attention to this emphasis on *echad* in Paul's writings and the failure to recognise it by Christian theologians. See: Wright, N T (1993) *The Climax of the Covenant: Christ and the Law in Pauline Theology,* Minneapolis, p125ff.

[81] Nassi, op.cit., provides an overview of the general issue.

Component p: the oath and the tree

If the last letter of *Elohim* is excluded, the result is:

p)   אֱלֹהִים

אֱלֹה   *aleph-lamed-hey   Ala*

This gives us the three letter word *ala (aleph-lamed-hey)* with the *yod* adding the possessive 'my' to that word. The Bible's main usage for *ala* is to mean a 'solemn oath', or the 'consequences of breaking an oath'. With the addition of the *yod*, the word *ala* becomes 'my' oath or 'my' consequences of breaking such an oath. It is mainly used of a covenant oath or the consequences of breaking such an oath. In Deuteronomy 29:12 and 14 Moses refers to the oath *(ala)* and the covenant that Israel is undertaking with the Lord. Given the necessary consequences of breaking such an oath, the oath and the consequences of breaking it are nearly identical for the party in breach.

Ala, with a different pronunciation *(eloha)*, can be used to refer to God and is related to the Islamic word for God, *Allah*. The Bible more frequently uses the plural term *Elohim*. Nonetheless, *ala* pronounced as *eloha* provides a close link between the name or nature of God and the other meanings of the word *ala*. This is a surprise: God will not be the party who breaks the covenant oath, so why would He link Himself in this way?

Some ancient Judaic scripts see a great oath as underlying creation.[82] In the context of Genesis 1:1 we can see *ala* as the oath that puts in place the covenant or as the consequences flowing from breaking that covenant. The consequence of breaking a covenant is that curses fall upon the covenant breaker. Deuteronomy 27 and 28 describe the many curses both individual and collective that will result from breaking the Mosaic covenant. Breaking covenant with God requires an offering to put the breach right. As described earlier, the sacrifice stands in the place of the covenant breaker and receives the curse instead.

The presence within *Elohim* of a word which can mean both 'my oath' and also 'my consequences of breaking covenant' suggests that *Elohim* Himself is directly involved not only in the making of a

---

[82] In the Apocrypha, Enoch 1 69:15-27 and Jubilees 36:7 (2nd or 1st Century BCE).

covenant but also in receiving the consequences of breaking it. These must be our consequences. If so, in some sense He receives a curse and. this must be on behalf of the covenant breakers, not for Himself.

There is a further meaning of *aleph-lamed-hey* in the Bible: pronounced *ela*, it means a 'strong tree' (from *el*, meaning 'strong') and is often translated as 'oak'. We have found two trees in the beginning: *ela* within *Elohim* and *berosh* within *beresheith*. These two different words for tree have slightly different meanings but they both speak of 'my tree'. In this case, 'my tree' is tied to 'my oath' and 'my consequences of breaking an oath'.

Ela is used in the sense of tree thirteen times in the *Tanach*. It is a place of danger or failure. It is where: Jacob hides foreign Gods (Genesis 35:4); David's errant son Absalom is caught by his hair and slain (2 Samuel 18: 9,10,14); an unnamed prophet is tricked (1 Kings 13:14); sacrifices are made to idols (Ezekiel 6:13; Hosea 4:13); and judgement occurs (Isaiah 1:30 and 6:13). Yet, something comes from this. Isaiah 6:13 refers to a faithful remnant of Israel, "a tenth portion" associated with the *ela* tree. The tree is burnt and casts off its leaves or is felled (the Hebrew is unclear), yet "the holy seed is its stump". The "holy seed" comes from that which appears dead: the burnt tree. Rebirth occurs at the tree. The burn tree and its holy seed remind us of the *berosh* tree that is on fire (component k) and the fruit that it produces.

Similarly, the word *ela* is the name of the valley where Israel faced defeat at the hands of Goliath until David uses his slingshot to kill the giant (1 Samuel 17). What all of Israel could not achieve, David – a type of the Messiah – did. [83]

The duality of the *ela* tree, which can point to disaster or to recovery, parallels the duality in the same letters when viewed as *ala*: it can mean either covenant oath or the consequences of breaking that oath. Again, it parallels the tree of component (k) that was connected with the sign for both divine power and for corruption.

Both trees in Genesis 1:1 are connected to a strong duality. Their presence in the first verse evokes the two trees in the Garden of Eden described in Genesis 2 and 3: the tree of life, which gave eternal life, and the tree of knowledge of good and evil. The nature and implication of these trees has been subject to much conjecture and is

---

[83] Isaiah 6:13 may point to Isaiah 11:1 which says "a shoot will spring from the stem of Jesse" and is usually seen as referring to David and to a future Messiah.

beyond our scope, though we may note the dualities also associated with the trees in the Garden.

Following the word *ala* is the remaining letter, *mem*. This takes the closed form used in Hebrew when the letter *mem* occurs at the end of a word, rather than the open form used when it occurs within or at the beginning of a word.

מ   *mem*

In symbolic terms, the letter *mem* in its closed form stands for the concealed part of God's rule or of His teaching in the Bible. It is sometimes held to refer to the Messiah.[84]   Here, the presence of the closed *mem* associates concealment with the consequences of breaking a covenant oath or with His strong tree. Why would such matters be concealed?   For example, the *Tanach* makes the consequences of breaking the covenant oath clear under the Mosaic covenant.

Component q: the sheaf of wheat and the entrance to the temple

Within the word *Elohim*, we find *aleph-lamed-mem (ilem)*.

q)   אלהים

אלם   *aleph-lamed-mem   Ilem*

The two letters skipped over *(hey-yod)* will be examined in the next component. The word *ilem* means to 'tie fast' or to 'bind', or a 'sheaf of wheat so bound'. It can also mean a 'person bound into silence', that is a person who is dumb or mute.

The binding of wheat returns us to the theme of sacrifice. Leviticus 23 instructs that in the two annual harvest festivals a sheaf (usually of wheat) is to be waved before the Lord in the temple as a "wave offering" of the first fruits of the harvest. Earlier we saw that

---

[84] *Talmud, Shabbat,* 104a and *Sanhedrin* 94a. *Ruth Rabbah* and David Kimchi talk of the closed *mem* as Messianic. The hidden nature of Messiah is also suggested by Isaiah 30:20 which, talking of the restoration of Israel, says "Your teacher shall hide himself no longer.".

the word *bar* (son) can mean 'grain' — as in the grain offering — and is also associated with the first fruits which are offered to the Lord.

Ilem, in the sense of a person bound into silence, points again to a hidden aspect. The connection in the word *ilem* between a person bound into silence and wheat that is bound suggests some parallel between the two. This reminds us that the son figure in *beresheith* is also connected to a figure associated with sacrifice and to a sheaf of wheat.

In the Bible, the word *ulam* or *eylam* — which means the physical entrance to the temple — is sometimes shortened, by dropping the *vav* or *yod*. It then becomes *aleph-lamed-mem*:[85]

אולם or אילם becomes אלם *Ulam*

These are the same letters, though pronounced differently, as *ilem*. Hence, the letters *aleph-lamed-mem* can indicate a sheaf of wheat or the entrance to the temple. What has a sheaf of wheat to do with the entrance to the temple? The connection is that when all Israel is commanded to come before the Lord in the temple at the harvest festivals and the feast of booths, they are instructed not to come before Him empty handed (Exodus 23:15, Deuteronomy 16:16). To go into the temple requires offerings to be brought. The waving of the sheaf of wheat and the other offerings provide the basis for entry into the temple. The *ilem* is the price for us to gain entry *(ulam)* to the place of His presence.

The physical temple in Jerusalem was founded upon a threshing floor, the place for the threshing of wheat. Earlier, the temple foundation was found in the first word (component (g) above). The physical temple in Jerusalem has gone but the opening of Genesis indicates that a foundation remains for us. This is through a sacrificial sheaf that gives us entry to the place of His presence.

At the entrance to the Bible is the entrance to the temple. Entry is gained by means of an offering. We enter into understanding the name of God as we enter into understanding the sacrifice that is provided for this purpose and that is described in the Bible's opening words.

---

[85] This occurs in its ten uses in Ezekiel 40 and in some variants or notations of 1 Kings 7.

Component r: the lamentation

Separating the *aleph-lamed* from the *mem* within the word *Elohim* are two letters *hey-yod*, giving us *hy:*

r)   אל**הי**ם

הי   *hey-yod*   *Hy*

The word *hy* is one of a group of similar sounding words – approximating the familiar 'oy' of Hebrew and Yiddish speakers – used interchangeably in the Bible to express woe or pain:

הי הוי הו הה אהה   or   אוי

To exclaim 'oy' or 'hy' in the beginning is strange coming from the all powerful Creator. God cries out 'oy' but what is He crying 'oy' about?

The setting gives us the answer. Within the word for Lord is woe: woe about the sacrifice needed to meet the covenant oath and gain entry to the temple. As the woe comes from within the sheaf, it is as if the sheaf itself laments. The woe of the silent victim in *Elohim* reflects that God identifies with this sacrifice and laments.

The Creator joins with us in the pain and suffering in the world. His engagement with us carries a price for Him. What we have found within the word *Elohim* suggest the nature of that price. He is taking on the consequences of oath (i.e. covenant) breaking by human beings on our behalf. His consequent woe leads to the closed *mem*, that is, to the concealed part of His rule. Component (q) connects this concealed rule with a person bound into silence.

That the Lord suffers with us should not be a shock. For example, in the face of Israel's sinfulness, Jeremiah 9:1 and 13:17 and Isaiah 22:4 describe how He suffers and weeps with Israel and *Beresheith Rabbah* suggests that He goes into exile with her (95:3). This is not some vague symbolism; the pain and cost are real. Jeremiah 9:2 finds Him longing to abandon His people, yet He cannot: the covenant is binding on both parties.

Isaiah 52 and 53 speak of a suffering servant. To quote from a paraphrase of Isaiah 53:5–6 by the 6th Century CE 'poet of the liturgy' Rabbi Eliezer Kalir in his prayer for *Yom Kippur* (the Day of Atonement): "He hath borne the yoke of our iniquities, and our transgression, and is wounded because of our transgression. He beareth our sins on his shoulder, that he may find pardon for our iniquities."[86] Verse 7 of Isaiah 53 refers to this servant as "like a lamb that is led to slaughter, like a sheep that is dumb before its shearers". The word "dumb" here is *ilem* (*aleph-lamed-mem*), that is component (q) above.

The 'suffering servant' passages of Isaiah have been subject to much debate as to whether they refer to an individual Messiah figure and / or Israel collectively.[87] We cannot join this debate. But, whatever the view taken, these passages clearly speak of iniquity leading to sacrificial loss that is focused upon a single party – a Messiah figure – whether that is Israel or an individual or individuals or some symbolic notion or figure. This chimes with our findings both from components within the word *beresheith* and those from within the word *Elohim*. We cannot resolve the precise interpretation of the Isaiah 53 passages here but this enquiry can deepen understanding of that which Isaiah writes. Indeed, we find this in the next component – 'the Lord who suffers' – which looks at the word *Elohim* as a whole.

Component s: the Lord who suffers

The *oy* of the Lord forms part of the word that introduces the Creator to us. Taking the word *Elohim* as a whole, we can look at it as combining the *mem* from component (p) with the woe of component (r) and the short expression for Lord: *El*. Dividing the word *Elohim* that way we obtain:

s) אל הי ם

Elohim is the Lord *(aleph-lamed)* whose suffering *(hey-yod)* is concealed *(mem)*. This is the nature of His name: the Lord whose suffering is concealed.

---

[86] From the *Musaf* service in the *Machzor Rabbah for the Great Day of Atonement*.
[87] The debate is beyond our scope. Hebraic sources that see some form of reference to an individual Messiah figure here include: *Talmud, Sanhedrin* 98a and b and *Mota* 14b; *Targum Yonathan, Beresheith Rabbah; Zohar* II:212a and III 218a; *Pesikta Rabbati* 36 – 37; *Midrash Tanchuma;* Ramban; Maimonides, Moses Alshech (Safed, Holy Land, 1508–1593); and, in the Dead Sea Scrolls, *Habakkuk Pesher* 1QpHab and fragment 4Q491c 1. Ramban and Maimonides also see Israel as the suffering servant, as do some earlier writers, and that is where the emphasis lies in more recent Judaic writings.

Looked at another way, the word *Elohim* consists of the two components (q) and (r).

אלם   and   הי

Together these two words tell us that *Elohim* is so closely connected to the sacrifice which provides entry to the temple that from the midst of this sacrifice bursts His lamentation or woe. Our entry to His presence is through a loss that the Lord Himself proclaims. The Lord is intimately involved, maybe through the figure bound in silence. This, too, is the nature of His name.

In addition to these ways of looking at the name of the Lord, we saw in component (p) that *Eloha* identifies the name of the Lord with (our) consequences of breaking the covenant oath.

These three different aspects of the name of the Lord *Elohim* (plural) or *Eloha* (singular) align with the results from examining the first word. Both tell us that God is involved in some hidden way with a sacrifice that is costly to Him. This is in the context of the temple of creation and covenant sacrifice. That story is not over. All this is hidden both in the beginning and in the name of the Lord. Again, "Indeed, You are a God who conceals Himself, the God of Israel is the Saviour" (Isaiah 45:15).

The problem of how creation can make adequate offering or restitution back to the Creator arose with the Abrahamic covenant. After Abram had cut the animals in two to make the necessary covenant sacrifice, "terror and great darkness fell upon him" (Genesis 15:12). Abram was wise to be depressed. How could a mere man, even Abram, undertake to fulfil a covenant with the Creator God. God resolved the problem by passing between the divided animals on behalf of both Himself and Abram and so undertook the covenant Himself (Genesis 15:17–18). Parallels are found at the beginning of creation.

Ramban analyses the word *Elohim* and finds in it the *El* (Lord) over all these, that is to say the Lord over all the forces of creation. He reads the remaining letters *hey-yod-mem* as indicating the Hebrew word *hey-mem* or *hey-mem-hey* which means 'these' or 'they'. Hence *Elohim* means 'Lord over these (forces)'. However, Ramban's approach falls outside the strict criteria of this enquiry. In the Hebrew Bible the word for 'these' or 'they' does not take on the form *hey-yod-mem.* and this enquiry only considers words in the form that they are found within the *Tanach*.

A final check is necessary on the use of the word *Elohim* in the first verse. Is there any form of word(s) connecting it to the following word in Genesis 1:1?

Unlike *bereseheith,* there are no evident words from Hebrew usage in the *Tanach* that can be deduced to span the gap. Indeed, there is no word acting as a bridge with either the preceding word or with the following word. *Elohim* stands on its own.

Summary: the Creator's heartbreak

Step six has considered the Divine. What emerges is surprising. The name *Elohim* can be seen as His cry of woe and a statement on the nature of His engagement with us.

Rabbi Nahaman saw the groans, the *oys,* of the sincere person as precious or holy, for they are laments over the absence or inaccessibility of God.[88] We have discovered the *oy* – the lamentation – of God over the price of making Himself accessible to us. This is the cry of His heart. We need to hear it.

The unity of the first name of God hints at a form of plurality but the implications are unclear.

We have looked at two ways of dividing *Elohim,* the word used most frequently for God in the Bible. Within His name we have found a word which means His covenant oath / the consequences of breaking such an oath / a strong tree. The tree is a place of both danger and hope. This tree can be said to represent God's perspective, whilst the previous tree within *beresheith* is connected to mankind's perspective.

A second word found within His name means a sheaf of wheat tied up or a person bound into silence. These meanings indicate a sacrifice which gains entry to the temple, that is to the presence of God, for us. From within the sheaf comes a lamentation.

Woe because of this loss is contained within the word *Elohim.* The *oy* of *Elohim* shows that He himself identifies with, and mourns over, the sheaf of wheat. The Creator is far from remote or retired from His creation. He participates with the covenant sacrifice to make the bonds that unite us with Him by bridging the divide between Creator and creation. His action is connected to a tree and / or a covenant oath and / or the consequences of breaking the covenant. This is not a distant, disengaged and rule making God.

---

[88] Rabbi Nahman of Bratizlava (1772–1810) in *Likkutei Moharan.*

All this is hidden. *Elohim* is the name of the Lord whose suffering is concealed. The word *Elohim* tells us that to see His loving kindness we need to look deep to find the Lord who laments in a hidden way, the one who cries in woe from amid the sacrifice. This begins to show us the nature of God's hiding that various Bible verses refer to. Later, we shall see that this hidden name is paralleled by two other names that lie within the first four words.

The pain of sacrifice to fulfil the requirements of covenant is reflected throughout the *Tanach*, as well as in the word *Elohim*. The Lord is not some generic God figure; He is specifically the God of Israel, and the God of Abraham, Isaac and Jacob. That is, He is the God of His covenant, first with Abraham, then with Isaac, then with Jacob, then with all of Israel. He is the God of relationship through covenant and of the cost of fulfilment of that covenant. He cares. And that is how it is set out in His name.

Elohim parallels *beresheith* in terms of what lies within. The plain text speaks of the first act of creation and thus the necessary distinction and separation between Creator and creation. Beneath this is a sub-text in both words which points to resolving this divide from the Creator's side. There is sacrifice and covenant and a figure that achieves this. But these words also speak of uncertainties, dualities and hidden-ness. The fourth word, to which we turn next, brings these concepts together. It gives us a sign that encompasses all.

Step Seven: The Sign

The fourth word, which leads to the bridge between Creator and creation and to *Elohim's* all encompassing sign to us.

The first three words resonate with each other. We come now to the last and smallest of the four words that open the Bible. The word is not translatable into English, yet tells us much. It speaks of a sign that is to all of creation, and that is from first to last. It provides the sign or seal for the opening to the Bible.

The third word, the term *Elohim*, is used of the Deity over 2,500 times in the *Tanach*. Often, a descriptive word is added: God of all the earth, God of the heavens, and so forth. At first glance, there is no descriptor here in its very first appearance in the Bible. The little word that follows *Elohim* supplies such a descriptor.

Component t: the little fourth word

The fourth – and also the sixth – word in the opening sentence of Genesis is *et*, a Hebrew preposition.

t) בראשית ברא אלהים אֵת

אֵת   *aleph-tav   Et*

The word in its application here is not directly translatable into English. It is used before the object of a sentence to confirm or emphasise that word as the object of the verb in the sentence, the thing that is acted upon. *Et* shows completion of the action described by the verb and serves to hold the words in clear association with each other. Here it is used to confirm that the heavens and the earth are indeed created by God.

In Hebraic thought, the *et* points to the substance or essence of the thing in view.[89] Here it is seen as showing the completion and perfection of the creative act of God. It shows that: "In the initial act of creation, the potential existed for all that will ever be contained in the universe."[90]

Et consists of the first and last letters of the Hebrew alphabet: *aleph* and *tav*. It speaks of the first and the last. Three times in the book of Isaiah, the Lord refers to Himself as the first and the last (Isaiah 41:4, 44:6, 48:12). It becomes part of the name of God and *Elohim* is identified with the first and the last. So it is in Genesis 1. Indeed, Isaiah 48:12–13 refers back to Genesis 1:

> Listen to Me, O Jacob, even Israel whom I called; I am He, I am the first, I am also the last. Surely My hand founded the earth, and My right hand spread out the heavens.

The *aleph-tav* is identified with the name of God in the beginning.

Genesis begins with the letter *bet* and we have seen that *bet* is connected to creation. It follows that the *aleph-tav* in Genesis 1 enfolds creation; it is both before and after creation. In bringing together the first and last letters of the Hebrew alphabet, the *aleph-tav* is seen in Hebraic thought as standing for the whole alphabet, and for the whole word of God. Its presence as the fourth word before the heavens and the earth are mentioned illustrates that the source of creation lies in the *aleph-tav*, the whole word of God.[91]

Psalm 119:89 says "Forever, O Lord, Thy word stands firm in the heavens." In Genesis 1:1 the first *aleph-tav* precedes the Hebrew word for heavens. This validates our quest to uncover a key to the whole in

---

[89] Ibn Ezra (Spain 12thC); David Kimchi, *Book of Roots,* (France, 1157–1236).
[90] *Talmud, Hagigah* 12a.
[91] Rabbi Dov Ber, *Or Torah,* 35. Dov Ber lived in Ukraine (c1710–1772).

the first words of the Bible. Whatever the key may be, it stands forever, firm in the heavens.

The letters *aleph-tav* can be used in Hebrew as a preposition meaning 'together with'. In these terms, the *aleph-tav* links the first half of Genesis 1:1 with the second half. It links God's act of creation with what is created: namely, the heavens and the earth. The components we have examined tell us of Divine action. What does this action relate to? It relates to what follows. The next letter in Genesis 1:1 is the letter *hey*. *Aleph-tav-hey* means 'you', that is us.[92] As we move from the first half of Genesis 1:1 to the second half, the focus moves from what God is doing to its implications for us and to our response. The *aleph-tav* is associated with *Elohim* and is a promise of the Creator's involvement with – of His 'together with' – His creation.

This leads on to our part in His plan. The 'together with' can operate in both directions. We must look both for "God with us" – how He comes near to us – and for how we can respond so that we draw near to Him. Genesis 1:1 tackles both aspects, as we shall see.

In the first verse of Genesis, the *aleph-tav* occurs both before the word for 'heavens' and before the word for 'earth'. The heavens and the earth are both equally subject to the action of the *aleph-tav*. They are both equally created by God, equally the subject of His creative power and of His order, and equally linked to Him. The realm of the material, the earthly, is not devalued.

By contrast, Greek and many other philosophies identify the realm of the ideal or rational or mathematical as standing far above the material world and determining it. Such philosophies place the material world – the earth – on a lower level than the heavens and often subsume the Divine into the heavenly. Genesis and the Hebraic mind set do not adopt that perspective and thus do not devalue flesh and blood or confuse some 'higher' element of creation with the Creator. Indeed, the only part of creation that is singled out in Genesis 1 as being close to the Creator is mankind, made from the dust of the earth yet created in His image.

The *tav* of *aleph-tav* recalls the *tav* that concludes *beresheith*, the first word in the Bible (component (m) above). On its own, the letter *tav*, as the last letter in the Hebrew alphabet, means 'conclusion'. Joined together, the *aleph* and the *tav* denote the wholeness of God's plan for creation from beginning to end. There is a beginning, there is an end and something else must happen in between.

---

[92] The *Zohar* I:115b notes this.

The association of *aleph-tav* with the first name of God in the Bible confirms that He becomes knowable to us by His action in history and that this action is directed towards His plan for history, from first to last. This plan is "together with" us.

Component u: the sign

The word *et* has a meaning in its own right. The Hebrew for sign consists of three letters: *aleph-vav-tav*. Often the *vav* is dropped, making the word for sign *aleph-tav*.[93]

u)   אות   *aleph-vav-tav*   *Owth*   or   את

Thus, *aleph-tav (et)* as a word can mean 'sign'. Since *aleph-tav* indicates the first and last, consequently its meaning as sign is as the sign of the first and last. Where can we find such a sign in the *Tanach?*

Exodus 4:8 speaks of a "first sign" and a "last (or second) sign", both times with the *vav* omitted. These refer to signs that Moses has been sent by God to save Israel out of Egypt. The second sign of Exodus 4:8 is sometimes seen as Messianic, pointing to the one who will save Israel, as Moses did.[94]

As it is both first and last, the sign of the *aleph-tav* is everlasting. There is one reference to an "everlasting sign" in the *Tanach.* Isaiah 55:13 speaks of an everlasting sign which the appearance of the cypress tree *(berosh)* and the myrtle provide.[95] Unexpectedly, the *berosh* tree discussed under component (k) is linked to the *aleph-tav* as an everlasting sign. The *berosh* and the *aleph-tav* are also woven together by the omission of the *vav* in their appearance in Genesis 1:1.

The omission of the letter *vav* – which symbolises completion – from the word for sign implies that this sign of completion is incomplete. The *aleph-tav* has a double reference: to a sign of the first

---

[93] In the *Torah,* the first five books of the Bible, the *vav* is omitted six times out of 22 occurrences of the singular form of "sign" and 11 out of 15 times with the plural form.

[94] See, for example, *Shemot Rabbah* 3c. (*Shemot Rabbah* is a *midrash* dating to 6th–9th Century CE.)

[95] Myrtle was the original name of Esther and is also associated with the joyous Feast of Tabernacles *(Sukkot).* It is a perfumed shrub used in the Middle East as a sign of jubilation, notably at weddings. Thus the everlasting sign is connected both with the *berosh* tree of sacrifice and the myrtle tree which is symbolic of rejoicing at being joined together.

and last which is everlasting and to a sign that is an incomplete completion. But a sign of what?

There are many signs from or of the Lord mentioned in the *Tanach*. However, there are two words that we have looked at which have specific connections with a sign from the Lord in the Bible. As we have just seen, the *berosh* (tree) is connected to an everlasting sign in Isaiah 55:13. This fits with the everlasting nature of the *aleph-tav* but leaves us puzzled as to what is going on.

Earlier we saw that there is a sign present for three of the four great expressions of covenant in the *Torah*: the covenants of Noah, Abraham and Moses. Each is introduced in terms of a sign: *owth* (with the *vav*). Only the later New Covenant has no sign explicitly specified for it in the Bible. Could the *aleph-tav* be the sign of a covenant? If so, it might refer to the sign of the rainbow in the Noetic Covenant, the sign of circumcision in the Abrahamic Covenant, the sign of the Sabbath in the Mosaic Covenant, the unknown sign for the New Covenant, or to some other expression of covenant.

Of these possibilities, we can identify which one the *aleph-tav* speaks to. The New Covenant is linked with beginnings, since the word 'new' *(chadash)* is associated with being first or at the start or beginning of something. The same root word is used for the new moon and consequently for the lunar month which begins with the new moon. The New Covenant is the covenant of the beginning.

The New Covenant is the last of the great God-given covenants mentioned in the *Tanach*. In Jeremiah 31, the New Covenant is described in terms of "days that are coming". It was yet to be uncovered or fulfilled when Jeremiah wrote, unlike the other covenants. Therefore, the New Covenant is associated with being both last and first: the sign of the first and the last is the sign of the New Covenant.

The sign of the *aleph-tav* is everlasting. Various covenants are described as everlasting in the *Tanach*. The New Covenant is spoken of as an everlasting covenant by Jeremiah in Jeremiah 32:37–41 and 50:4–5. These and other passages (Isaiah 42:6, 61:8; Ezekiel 16:60–63)[96] look to the establishment of a covenant relationship that lay in the future when they were written.

While this future hope helps explain the setbacks and confusion of the present age, there seems to be a further contradiction here, as with the incomplete completion. If the sign is both first and last, how can it denote a New Covenant that was preceded by other expressions of

---

[96] Also the 2nd Century BCE apocryphal writing, the book of Baruch 2:30-35.

covenant between God and humanity? That is not first. And how can a New Covenant be everlasting if it had not begun when Jeremiah wrote? We shall begin to see the resolution in the next step. Ecclesiastes 1:10 provides a hint:

> Is there anything of which one might say: "See this, it is new"? Already it has existed for ages which were before us.

There is a further question about the connection between the New Covenant and the other statements of covenant. The Abrahamic, Mosaic and New Covenants are all made with Israel. The Abrahamic and Mosaic covenants were fulfilled by earthly sacrifices that stood in our place and under the Mosaic covenant these were undertaken in an earthly temple. We should expect a real, earthly fulfilment of the New Covenant. What exactly is the sign of the New Covenant and how is it associated with the other covenants and with Israel? What is the sacrifice that stands in our place?

The location of this covenant and of the sign of the *aleph-tav* at the beginning of creation indicates that the covenant and sign are foundational. As the *aleph-tav* can mean 'together with', this covenant provides for that 'together with' between God and man and, through us, with the rest of creation. This sign precedes Abraham, Israel and Moses and all the explicit statements of covenant in the Bible.

Passages in the *Tanach* hint of an everlasting covenant that goes wider than the relationship expressed through the Noetic, Abrahamic or Mosaic statements of covenant. Cain and Abel make sacrifices to the Lord and Abel's blood sacrifice is accepted. In Jeremiah 33:25 the Lord says "If My covenant for [with] day and night stand not, and the fixed patterns of heaven and earth I have not established, then I would reject the descendents of Jacob and David My servant..."[97] This statement links Israel's relationship with the Lord to a covenant which goes back to the creation account in the first verse of the Bible and projects forward into the future: a covenant that stretches from first to last. The covenant of the *aleph-tav* can be said to embrace all creation since the beginning. The great oath underlying creation that is referred to in the Apocrypha[98] may undergird this creation covenant and is reflected in the presence of the word *ala* (oath) in Genesis 1:1

---

[97] See also *Talmud Pesahim* 68b. Hosea 6:7 and Isaiah 24:5 refer to a covenant with humanity, though in some Judaic thinking this is understood to refer to Israel. In Deuteronomy 29:13-14/14-15 Moses makes a covenant and oath (*ala*) "with those who stand with us here today" and "with those who are not here with us today".

[98] See footnote 82.

(component (p) above). The Lord expresses His loving kindness from the beginning. Psalm 136 attaches the phrase "for His loving kindness endures forever" to events in creation week as well as in Israel's history.

What can this mean? The other statements of covenant in the *Tanach* mark the development of the relationship between the Creator and humanity, and more specifically Israel. As we shall see, this focus is not set aside with the New Covenant.

Jeremiah 31:32 contrasts the New Covenant with the Mosaic covenant: "My covenant which they broke". Similarly, Ezekiel 16:60–63 distinguishes sharply between a future covenant which sees the restoration of Israel and 'your covenant' (presumably the Mosaic covenant) which does not. The distinction suggests that the New Covenant puts things right in a way that does not occur under the other covenants. This must be the future aspect of the New Covenant. This sign and covenant have a past aspect that goes back to the beginning of creation and a future aspect looking forward to a putting right. However, we still do not know how this is to be fulfilled.

When the Abrahamic Covenant was cut, God passed in between the divided animal offerings – passing through their blood poured out on the ground – and sealed the covenant on behalf of both Abram and Himself. With the covenant in Genesis 1, God's direct involvement is shown by the presence of the word *ala* (meaning oath or breach of oath) within the word *Elohim*. The *ala* shows the Lord making a covenant oath and instigating a covenant, the New Covenant. *Elohim* takes on the consequences of our breach of covenant oath and puts it right by providing a sacrifice. Under the Mosaic covenant, temple sacrifices were required to make things right whilst the Jerusalem temple still stood. Under the New Covenant, one action by the Lord suffices. It is fulfilled by the sacrifice outlined in Genesis 1:1 that occurs in the temple of all creation. When and what is this?

Some rabbinical commentaries associate the New Covenant with the future coming of the Messiah and the son of God referred to in Psalm 2:7.[99] *Pesiqta Rabbati* 36 speaks of "my righteous Messiah, you took all this (that is sin) upon yourself from the six days of creation." The *aleph-tav* brings the Messiah figure together with covenant. As the fourth word in the Bible, the *aleph-tav* connects the covenant sacrifice identified in the three preceding words with the heavens and the earth

---

[99] For example, see *Midrash Tehilim*, 3, 4 and *Midrash Talpiyot*, 58a. (The *Tehelim* dates from 9–10th Century CE. The *Talpiyot* is a collection of *midrashim* by Eliyahu Ha Kohen of the 18th Century CE.) The Dead Sea Scrolls also expect the New Covenant to be realized through the Messiah.

mentioned next. This sign of the New Covenant points to the head of the house, the son and Messiah, fulfilling covenant by taking on the sacrificial role of the first fruits on behalf of the heavens and the earth. This brings woe to God (component (r) above).

The picture is reinforced by the grain offering discussed under components (h) and (q). Leviticus 2 specifies two requirements for the grain offering: it shall be anointed with oil, and it shall contain no leaven. Leaven is a symbol of sin and the term Messiah means anointed one in Hebrew. Hence, the grain offering suggests a Messiah figure that is without sin is associated with covenant sacrifice.

Human sacrifice is strictly forbidden in the *Tanach*. The incident when Abraham is saved from having to sacrifice his son Isaac (Genesis 22) underlines that the ram provided in his stead is a substitute. Hence, another seeming contradiction emerges from Genesis 1:1. Such sacrifice is not desired by God but could be suggested here by the combination of hints. We will return to this question in the next step.

The involvement of a Messiah figure in covenant sacrifice is also hinted at in Daniel 9:26 which says "Messiah will be cut off". The Hebrew word used here *yikareth* means 'he will be cut off' and derives from the root word *karath*. The primary use of *karath* in the Bible is in the sense of 'to cut' a covenant, since sacrificial animals are cut up as part of the covenant procedure. In Genesis 15:18, the Lord "cuts" *(karath)* a covenant with Abram. Daniel 9:26 implies that the Messiah may be so 'cut'.

Does this change Israel's position or responsibility? The covenants after Noah are with Israel but this does not imply that Israel on her own can either meet their conditions (and the *Tanach* records that she does not) or should herself be the sacrifice to cover that lack (and the *Tanach* records that she should not be). The covenant oaths and the lives of the patriarchs of Israel demonstrate this.

Despite her failures, Israel remains in covenant relationship with the Creator. She is a focus for God's creative activity and is His firstborn and first fruits. The Lord says "I will also walk among you and be your God and you shall be My people." (Leviticus 26:12). Israel is chosen to be a kingdom of priests and a holy nation (Exodus 19:6) and the *kedusha* prayer of Judaism begins "we will make Your name holy in the world".

The effect of the covenants extends out from Israel. Abraham was told "in you all the families of the earth shall be blessed" (Genesis 12:3) and both the Abrahamic and Mosaic covenants make provision for foreigners. When the Mosaic Covenant was given to Israel, those foreigners who were with Israel could join with Israel under the covenant and its authority. Isaiah 42:6 says of "My servant", "I will appoint you as a covenant to the people, as a light to the nations." (Similarly Isaiah 49:6–8.) In Hebrew, the term 'people' *(am)* in the singular means a specific group rather than people in general. In context, this is necessarily Israel, whilst the reference to "nations" is to all others, that is to the gentiles. The covenant is with Israel; the light is to the nations (gentiles) in general. Likewise, the New Covenant is given first to Israel (Jeremiah 31:31). The covenants are expressed through Israel outward to the nations. Kindness to strangers is commanded (Leviticus 19:34, Exodus 23:9 and elsewhere). Similarly, when Israel fails it is "in the sight of the nations" (Ezekiel 36). Israel's job is to serve as a witness and messenger of the covenant that links humanity with God: "For My house will be called a house of prayer for all the peoples." (Isaiah 56: 7)[100]

But, if the covenant referred to in the beginning is with Israel, how can Israel be there in the beginning? There is a further problem. Under the Mosaic covenant, God's presence was focussed on the Ark of the Covenant in the physical temple at Jerusalem. These are long gone and Israel is warned in the *Tanach* against making offerings elsewhere. If we are to proceed under the New Covenant, where can His presence be found and what sacrifice can be offered there? We have both a problem of origin and a problem of maintaining the covenant. How can the Messiah figure resolve these?

Summary: the sign

The *aleph-tav* of Genesis 1:1 confirms the heavens and the earth as the subject of *Elohim's* creative act and the absolute divide between Creator and creation. The same two letters point to the bridge between Creator and creation that is laid down from the Creator's side: the sign of *Elohim* that embraces all of creation. The *aleph-tav* proclaims both the separation and the unification of Creator and creation. The unification is through the sign that is in the beginning: the first and last.

The word *Elohim* is often followed by a word that describes a particular aspect of *Elohim*. The *aleph-tav* describes *Elohim* here in its first appearance. It describes the nature of God. He is first and last, in

---

[100] Commenting on Isaiah 56:7-8, Rahsi sees that many gentile converts will rally to the Messiah.

the beginning and at the completion of His creation, and acting in time together with us.

The *aleph-tav* is the sign of the New Covenant. The New Covenant, by its name, is the covenant of the beginning. The New Covenant provides a basis for relationship upward to God and outward from Israel to the nations. It provides for a 'together with' between God and man. This is still incomplete and the *aleph-tav* is also the sign of the end and completion.

Step seven completes our word by word examination of the first four words of Genesis. The enquiry has shown that the second and fourth words mirror each other in that they both carry the idea of the movement of time from first to last. Similarly, the first and third words mirror each other in that they both carry references to suffering, sacrifice, dualities, hidden-ness and a tree.

From the Hebrew of these four words, the enquiry has unfolded some twenty distinct words with over thirty different meanings (summarised in Appendix B). Various Hebrew letters have also been examined, where these stand alone or modify the significance of the words found. We have been confronted by an unavoidable tension and discovered puzzles and hints as to a resolution. The solution remains a mystery; it looks to face irresolvable difficulties.

The remaining steps adopt two new approaches. These demonstrate how the many different pieces fit together and lead towards a founding reality.

Step Eight: Hidden Names

The hidden names within the first four words that encapsulate and express what has gone before and speak of the Creator's loving kindness.

W hat more appropriate statement to begin the book of books than a name or names foundational to understanding the Creator? In pre-modern cultures, names and titles matter; they state the fundamentals of who a person is and show their social standing.

Our word by word survey of the first four words is complete. This step looks at ways of reading these words in combination. Hidden name or titles of *Elohim* were revealed in step six, telling us of the Lord who suffers in a concealed way. Two further names can be discerned hidden within the first four words of Genesis when these words are taken as a whole. Their primacy of place gives them the utmost importance.

The two names that are revealed demonstrate a unity that encompasses the disparate components examined so far. The various words and concepts that we have found produce an intricate structure. Like an archaeological excavation, as separate discoveries are assembled the larger construct to which they belong becomes evident. A structure emerges which confirms what we have found and brings it together. The nature of the whole begins to appear.

In the *Tanach* names speak of identity. The various names of God are revelations of the Divine nature.[101] Each name describes attributes of God. In Exodus 3:13, Moses is concerned that when he tells Israel that the God of their fathers has sent him, they will ask "what is His name?" (that is, "who is He?") If there is a name of God to be uncovered in Genesis 1:1, it would tell us much of the nature of God. It would state His primary characteristic(s) towards His creation.

The Lord responds to Moses "*Ehyeh asher Ehyeh*": "I am that I am" or more properly "I will be that I will be". By this, He shows His ongoing and future involvement with us. In verse 15, the Lord says "This is My name forever". The Hebrew word 'forever' is here spelt the same way as the root word for concealed. God's name is hidden and Hebrew sages have deduced that the name of God spoken to Moses is not to be fully pronounced except in the temple. The verse also suggests that there is a hidden name or names of God in the Bible and consequently there is something hidden about His character.

What better place to hide such a name and thus to uncover more about His character than in the first words? The *Zohar* remarks that the entire *Torah* is composed of the names of God and the *shimoshi* branch of *Kabbalah* searches for hidden names of God by esoteric methods. [102] Without employing such methods, what can be found within the opening words of Genesis that yields a further name or names of God and tells us more about Him? One scholar has said "In every generation didst Thou make plain parts of the mystery of Thy name."[103]

The method we have adopted is straightforward and consists of reading the sixteen letters of the first four words in their existing order. Remember in the original *Torah* scrolls there is no pointing to indicate vowels and no spacing between words. The four words strictly are a succession of sixteen letters. Hence:

בראשיתבראאלהימאת[104]

---

[101] For example, the 5th Century CE *midrash, Rabbah Vayikrah,* says that the Lord redeems by His name (23.2).

[102] *Zohar Yisro* 87a. The Kabbalistic text *Sefer Yetzirah* proposes that the creation of the world was achieved by the manipulation of the sacred letters that form the names of God.

[103] *Siddur* of the Saadia Gaon (882–942, Egypt and Syria), p379 of the Davidson, Assaf and Yoel 1941 edition.

[104] As mentioned under point (p), the symbol for the Hebrew letter *mem* מ takes a different form when at the end of words: ם. Hence, the change in form of *mem,* the third from left Hebrew letter in our phrase, from ם to מ and back again.

Component v: the first name

Let us apply a different spacing than that used normally. This is not to suggest that the conventional reading is in any way in error. Based on the preceding discussion, there are two patterns. First:

v) בר אשית ברא אלהים את

In this arrangement, the second Hebrew word (reading from the right) is a variation on the word *sheth* discussed earlier under component (i) which means 'I (will) appoint' or 'I (will) place'.

The combination of words can be read as

> The son I appoint to creation, *Elohim*, the first and the last

The son is appointed to creation; by implication he is in charge. The titles *Elohim* and 'the first and the last' apply either to the son so appointed or to the one appointing him, that is, to God.

Earlier, we saw that God appoints His head to creation (component (d) above). This is underlined by the name we have found here. The son is that head and intermediary linking God and creation. Again, the son is presented as the bridge of the gulf between Creator and creation. A bridge is laid down from the Creator's side and it is 'the son I appoint'. This is the Creator's first and foremost action.

The word *barah*, translated above as 'creation', can in the context of Genesis 1:1 also be understood to mean 'creating' (the view, for example, of Rashi). In that case, the words read:

> The son I appoint to creating, *Elohim*, the first and the last

The creative power of God can be understood as flowing through the son. The son is the expression or realization of that power.

Sheth, the word translated as 'appoint', also refers to Eve's Messianic hope, as we saw earlier. This ties the son to the *sheth* figure. The son is appointed to creation and fulfils Eve's hope: the Messiah figure who brings God and man together. As we have argued, this is through covenant sacrifice. The *Talmud* tells us that the name of the Messiah shall endure forever and was ordained before creation. Here he is named before the heavens and the earth. By connection to the *sheth* figure, he is linked both to the Messianic hope and to the seat of judgement where that figure is appointed to sit.

The opening words of the Bible yield a name of God which ties together many of the components previously considered. This name of

God shows the son to be the creative power of God in creation, appointed there as the bridge between man and God. He is our Messianic hope who also may sit in judgement between the first and second creations. But, there is more.

Component w: the second name

There is another way of reading the first four words and this reading explains the nature of the mediation between Creator and creation that the son is appointed to. It shows us the title of the son:

w)   בר א שית בר א אלהים את

     bar aleph Sheth bar aleph Elohim aleph tav

This yields a text that can be read:

> Son – *Aleph* – Sheth (the son of man). Son – *Aleph* – God the first and the last (the sign)

Setting aside the 'spare' *alephs* for a moment, we have:

> Son, son of man, son of God, the first and the last

This also is a title or name. The combination of the two titles 'son of man' and 'son of God' in one phrase here in the beginning is striking. This combination does not occur in the plain text of Genesis 1, yet on closer examination we find that the son figure is joined both with man and with God. The *Targum Neofiti* picks up one element of this for it translates Genesis 1:1 as "From the beginning with wisdom the son of the Lord created and perfected the heavens and the earth."

The significance of the terms 'son of man' and 'son of God' has been debated. We cannot pursue that discussion in depth here. There are various references to God having a son (singular) in the Bible.[105] In Hebraic thought, these have been identified as Messianic: the Messiah had especially or peculiarly the characteristic of being the son (singular) of God.[106]

---

[105] Psalm 2:7 (and, debatably, verse 12), Psalm 89:27, Proverbs 30:4, Isaiah 9:6, Daniel 3:25 and, in the Apocrypha, 4 Ezra 7:28 (probably 1st Century CE).
[106] For example, on Psalm 2 see *Talmud, Sukkah* 52a, Rashi, Ibn Ezra, *Midrash Tehelim* fol.3, col.4, and *Yalqut* 2, 71. (The *Yalqut* is a c13th Century CE collection of *midrashim*.) The Dead Sea Scrolls use "son of God" in a Messianic way at fragment 4Q246.

By contrast, the term 'son of man' is mostly used of ordinary human beings in the *Tanach* but there has been Messianic conjecture around the title, based particularly on its use in Daniel 7:13 and, in the Apocrypha, 1 Enoch and 4 Esdras. 1 Enoch 62:7 says that this son of man is concealed from the beginning and later revealed, tying in with the reference to a son of man we have found literally hidden "in the beginning" *(beresheith)*. Daniel speaks of "one like a son of man" who is presented before "the Ancient of Days" and given authority, glory and kingship. The Talmud takes this as referring to the Messiah, as does Rashi, whilst the *Targums* translate the term "son of man" as "Messiah" here and in some of its other occurrences.[107]

The combination of the titles 'son of man' and 'son of God' in the first verse of Genesis clearly has Messianic implications and connects these titles to the Creator and His act of creation.

The two names hidden within Genesis 1:1 that we are discussing incorporate the title 'the first and the last'. As we have seen, *resheith* (beginning) also means first fruits or firstborn. There are several Messianic references to the firstborn or only son. The only son who is mourned at Amos 8:10 and Zechariah 12:10 is understood as the Messiah, as is the Lord's firstborn son in Psalm 89:27 who is described as "the most exalted of the kings of the earth".[108] We can say that the son, Messiah, is the firstborn son or first fruits of God. As the *Talmud* states "all the prophets prophesied only for the days of Messiah".[109] But this firstborn son also is connected to or has the characteristic of being last: he is both first and last.

Either there are two sons referred to here in Genesis 1 or there is one son who takes on aspects of both the human and the divine. The two references to son, both with Messianic implications, chime with the Hebraic understanding of two Messiahs.[110] One view is that first comes a Messiah of suffering and poverty: *Messiach ben* (son of) *Yosef.* This Messiah may be Israel. Later comes a Messiah of kingship who rules Israel: *Messiach ben* (son of) *David.* This approach unifies the

---

[107] *Talmud, Sanhedrin* 98a. The *Targums* in Psalms 8:4, 80:18, and 144:3.

[108] See *Talmud, Sukkah* 52a on the "only son" of Amos and Zechariah. *Shemot Rabbah* 19 refers to "Messiah, my firstborn" on the basis of Psalm 89:27. The Messiah king is seen in Psalms 21 and 72 by the *Targum Pseudo-Yonathan* and *Targum Yerushalmi.*

[109] *Talmud, Berakoth* 34b; similarly *Talmud, Sanhedrin* 99a.

[110] The *Talmud, Sukkah* 52 and *Sanhedrin* 98a say or imply that there will be two Messiahs; similarly *Ruth Rabbah* 5:6 and many rabbinic writings.

Scriptures that emphasise a Messiah of poverty and suffering with those that emphasise a Messiah of kingship.

The context of Genesis 1 suggests that one son fulfils the roles of both *Messiach ben Yosef* and *Messiach ben David*. The one son provides the bridge between Creator and creation being both son of man and son of God. That is the point of connection across the gulf. If there are two sons, then the name 'son, son of man, son of God, the first and the last' becomes incoherent. As we saw in step five, the son figure of the first verse is connected to both the first and the second creation. If there are two different sons here, then the connection and history between the two creations is lost. Nor would two different sons align with the son within the name 'the son I appoint to creation, *Elohim*, the first and the last.'

The thrust of the first four words points to a unity and under-girding for all of creation and all of history in one son and Messiah. That is why these words are placed first. If there is one son, then that son is both 'of man' and 'of God'. As this double character is specified in the beginning, it must be critical. Perhaps too there is a connection to the other dualities previously identified.

Along with the two references to son in the first verse of Genesis, there are also two appearances of a tree in components (k) and (p). Two different Hebrew words, with different connotations, are used for the two trees. The ordinary conifer tree *berosh* encompasses the first son. This tree is linked both to Divine power and to corruption. Occurring within the word for creation, it may represent the human perspective. The strong tree *ela* is found within *Elohim* and follows mention of the second son. It is linked to both a Divine oath and to the consequences of breaking an oath. This could represent the Divine perspective. The fruit of both trees is bitter: that of the conifer tree is fit for the fire, whilst that of the strong tree produces woe for God. The two trees illustrate how the son of *beresheith* and the son of *Elohim* – as well as the sacrifice hinted at in both words – may be one son and connected to one sacrifice, though viewed from different perspectives.

If the two hidden names we have discussed concern a single figure, there is a difficulty. We have understood *sheth* in the sense of a Messiah figure. Applying that understanding here, we obtain 'son of Messiah' rather than 'son of man'. This leads to a contradiction: Messiah equates to son of Messiah. We argue for a different reading. This enquiry has revealed layers of meaning and the same words or letters fulfilling several different functions. That results from the intense compression involved in the encoding that we are unpacking.

The understanding of *sheth* as Messiah helped unpack the meanings within the first word. The understandeith of *sheth* in the generic sense of mankind has helped us grasp a name hidden within the opening words. The two understandings occur in different contexts but both contribute to the entry code and compliment each other in that. There is no need to read 'son of Messiah' here.

The names or titles uncovered in Genesis 1:1 are the first in the Bible. They have pride of place. The names:

> Son, son of man, son of God, the first and the last

and

> The son I appoint to creation, *Elohim*, the first and the last

both encompass the word *Elohim*, the name of God in its first appearance. That name on its own can also mean:

> The Lord whose suffering is concealed.

Eloha, the singular form of *Elohim* contained within *Elohim*, means:

> Covenant oath / the consequences of breaking covenant oath

These four names combine together to express the identity the Creator reveals towards His creation: the covenant keeping God of Israel.

The reference to the heavens and the earth as that which is created occurs after these names. Their appearance is a later or subordinate event. The title of 'the first and the last' makes clear that the son of God, son of man, is not simply a part of creation but in some sense precedes, succeeds and encompasses creation. We should not be surprised. In the *Talmud* and Judaic writings, the name of Messiah has been seen as joined to the name of God and as existing before the foundation of the world.[111]

At the centre of the first act of creation is the son, Messiah figure. The word for son is placed within the word for creation and within the word for beginning. In its first occurrence it is connected to the earthly

---

[111] *Talmud Baba Bathra* 75b joins Messiah with the high name of God, YHWH, on the basis of Jeremiah 23:5–6. See also: *Beresheith Rabbah* 1:4; *Eichah Rabbah* 1:16 and 1:51 (4th-6th Century CE); *Mishle Rabbah* 10:21 and 10:24 (c8th Century CE); *Zohar* I:31a and 245b; and, in the Apocrypha, 1 Enoch 48:2-4 (which refers to the son of man in this way) and 3 Enoch 15: 73 and 76. In the *Tanach*, Micah 5:2 refers to "one [who] will go forth for Me to be ruler of Israel. His goings forth are from long ago, from the days of eternity." *Targum Yonathan* and the *Jerusalem Talmud, Berakoth* 5a take this as Messianic. See also footnote 70.

Sheth. In its second occurrence, it is connected to the Divine. A Messiah is appointed who is connected both to God and to man. The name found hidden within the word *Elohim* must similarly refer to this Messiah: he is that lord who suffers in a concealed way.

As son of man, son of Sheth, he replaces Abel, who was murdered for his blood sacrifice, and fulfils Eve's Messianic hope. He also succeeds Abel's murderer, Cain. He takes on both the priestly role of Abel and the corruption of Cain. As son of God, the Messiah provides the metaphysical aspect lacking in the earthly Sheth. The *yod*, representing the metaphysical, is lacking in the earthly Sheth but present in the *sheth* of Genesis 1. This points to the Messiah figure combining both the earthy and the metaphysical: he is both son of man and son of God. As son of God, the son connects us to God and in a way that, as son of man, can be grasped by us. These two characteristics of the son provide the vital link between Creator and creation that maintains the Creator's creation project.

This works through covenant sacrifice. If he represents us in the place of sacrifice, then he takes on our corruption – illustrated by Cain – so that it is consumed in the sacrificial fire. He can act as an offering on behalf of Israel, of all humanity and indeed of all creation. His sacrifice mediates between God and us in the New Covenant.

How can this be, since human sacrifice is explicitly forbidden in the *Tanach*? However, there is no breach of this rule. The New Covenant and the associated arrangement over a sacrificial offering precede all the other covenants and in particular the rules about sacrifice under the Mosaic covenant. This sacrifice is determined by the Creator and not imposed by us on anybody. As both son of God and son of man, the Messiah moves beyond the boundaries applying to others. That the Messiah will bear the sins of other and die a sacrificial death are not unknown concepts within Judaism. [112]

The covenant sacrifice of the Messiah also fits with the clues we have uncovered in previous steps. Messiah is the first fruits required for sacrifice and that stands in the place of all that follows. Messiah is the fruit of the tree consumed by fire, the head that becomes desolate, the gift of homage broken in judgement, the appointed one subject to shame, the sheaf of wheat that is the price of entry to the temple and that causes God woe.

---

[112] For example, *Pesikta Rabbati* 35 states that the patriarchs will come in the month of Nissan to the Messiah and say "you are greater than us because you have borne the sins of our children". Concepts of the Messiah are discussed further in step ten and see also the references there in footnotes 136 and 138.

Without the covenant sacrifice spoken of in the beginning, there can be no enduring relationship with the Creator and thus no basis for creation to continue to exist. That is why this matter is mentioned first in the Bible. From the beginning, the heavens and the earth look forward to this fulfilment. It takes the Messiah to provide it.

If we look at the whole of Genesis 1:1 and use *aleph-tav* in the sense of 'together with' rather than 'first and last', then the two names of God tell us that the figure of the son is together with the heavens and together with the earth. He is the bridge between Creator and creation and sits amid creation. In the figure of the son we have found the fulfilment of Messianic hope and the full name of *Elohim*.

This explains how names that refer to a son can be given such primacy of place. In Islam there is a statement of recent origin: "God has no need of a son to manage His affairs".[113] We have found that God has need of a son, not in order to manage His affairs but to rescue us from ours; to bridge the gulf that lies between us and our Creator. The Creator makes Himself known to us through His son.

Summary: Hidden names

God reveals Himself and lays bare his character in the opening verse of the Bible. The names we have found there are the first and most fundamental expression of who the Creator is in relation to His creation. They encompass all the previous components and the hints that we have uncovered and give expression to the hidden, eternal and forward looking name and character that God reveals towards His creation. This centres on the covenant sacrifice of the Messiah.

These names help us to understand two different aspects of God's activity in creation: the 'I' who appoints and the one who is appointed. The two names that span the first four words – the son of God appointed to creation and the son of God, son of man, the first and the last – provide the foundation for understanding the God who speaks through the Biblical narrative. In addition, we saw earlier that *Elohim* is the name of the Lord whose suffering is concealed and *Eloha* identifies the Lord with the covenant oath.

This son looks forward to the future as well as back to the creation and is tied into the Messianic hope for resolving the troubles

---

[113] The phrase was coined by Abdullah Yusuf Ali (1872–1953), an Islamic scholar who translated the *Quran* into English. It does not come from the *Quran* or other Islamic holy writings.

of the present world. He is placed in the past, the present, and the future.

The names we have found are an expansion or explication of *Elohim*. *Elohim* is the name of God acting in creative power to create the heavens and the earth. Therefore, these names expand or explicate the application of that creative power by the Creator. They could be said to hint at what is involved: how God 'does' creation, so to speak.

In Hebraic understanding, the first use of a word or term in the Bible is a key to understanding it. Similarly, a short reference to a word or phrase implies the fuller explication provided earlier in the text. Hence, every time the term *Elohim* is used of the Lord, it implies this first instance. Over 2,500 times, the Bible implies the expansions of *Elohim* hidden in Genesis 1:1.

This distinguishes *Elohim* when used of the Deity from *elohim* when used of earthly lords or of other gods. Only *Elohim* used of the one God has these additional meanings. They give us the title of the Lord of creation: the Lord engaged with His creation through covenant sacrifice, and who suffers in a concealed way. No other lord and no other god can claim this. We have found the fountainhead of the many images and associations hidden in the Bible to help us seek Him.

The next step will show us how to seek Him by means of two threads woven through the opening words.

Step Nine: The Barest Breath

Two threads woven through the design. One speaks of the
presence of God and the other speaks of a surprising absence.

T he breath of God in creation can be heard in the opening words if
    we listen carefully.   Step nine considers two threads woven
through the opening words of Genesis that help draw together what
has gone before. One thread speaks of a presence, and the other of an
absence. Together they bring into focus the underlying dynamic of
what we have uncovered.

Steps one to seven examined the first four words in depth, at
times letter by letter. With the eighth step we stood back and looked
for a message within the phrase taken as a whole. With steps nine and
ten we look for patterns contained within that phrase. Solely to look
for patterns of letters in the Hebrew Bible would be a dubious exercise,
even when confined to the first few words. However, this enquiry
provides an anchor and reference point through its method and the
findings from the approaches used in the previous steps. The patterns
that emerge in this and the final step are subtle but persistent. They
take us deeper.

Like the repetition of notes or the absence of expected notes in a
piece of music, they give focus and force to what we are hearing.
Because the patterns stretch across the four words, they weave the
whole together. Each step and each level provides clarification of what

has gone before. Observing the strict rules stated at the outset, we continue to extract the information encoded within the first four words so as to hear the barest breath of God.

Component x: the spare alephs

As we have noted, the Bible begins with a *bet,* the second letter of the Hebrew alphabet, not with the *aleph,* the first letter. At the same time, we have repeatedly encountered 'spare' *alephs* within the opening words. For example, the second of the two names of God looked at in step eight contains two 'spare' *alephs:*

x)   בר א שית בר א אלהים את

   The two *alephs* each separate the word for son from, respectively, the word for *sheth* or man and from the word for God. Previously we found a 'spare' *aleph* within the word for 'my tree', where it separates the word for son from the word for gift of homage. We found a spare *aleph* when the first and second words were brought together to refer to that gift as broken in judgement. In sum, we have:

- the *aleph* in the midst of the son of man;

- the *aleph* in the midst of the son of God,

- the *aleph* in the midst of the tree

- the *aleph* connected with a gift of homage broken in judgement.

In each case the *aleph* can be thought of as added to or surplus to the word concerned or hidden within the word or trapped by it. What do these *alephs* tell us?

   As mentioned under component (k), the letter *aleph* by itself can represent God or the connection between God and man. The implication of the 'spare' *alephs* in Genesis 1:1 is twofold. First: when we look at the world that He has created, the presence of God may not seem to fit in. There may be no evident presence of the Lord or connection with Him, and we might imagine that He is not there or that He has withdrawn and stands outside our story. Second: He is present with us in His creation through the son-Messiah figure, but that is hidden. We have discussed His hidden names and seen the concealed part of God's rule or teaching. He has not withdrawn from us, though He may be hidden.[114]

These implications of the 'spare' *alephs* tie in with the ordinary function of the *aleph* in pronouncing Hebrew words. The *aleph* signals the breath taken in preparation for pronouncing the following sound. It provided a short pause and gives emphasis to the pronunciation of the next letter. So, in pronouncing Hebrew, the *aleph* itself is the barest breath; it is hidden and lends its power to another letter or group of letters rather than drawing attention to itself. The first letter in the Hebrew alphabet – which can stand for God Himself – hides. In these first uses of the *aleph* in the Bible, we see how the Creator hides Himself from His creation, yet remains engaged.

This veiling is like the veiling of His presence in the Ark of the Covenant. The Ark was the focus for God's presence in the Jerusalem temple, but was hidden from ordinary human eyes. The opening words of the Bible prompt us to realize that His hidden presence is woven into creation. But where in particular can He now be found?

The *aleph* as the hidden breath of God is different from the explosive blowing of His breath *(neshamah)* into the nostrils of Adam that gave Adam life, as described in Genesis 2:7. The breath of the *aleph* is gentle, not forceful. Life was imparted to Adam by the blowing of the breath of the Creator, but the *aleph* of the Creator must be searched out. The pattern of 'spare' *alephs* helps us to do this.

The plain sense of the letter *aleph* is the first person singular: 'I'. Used as a suffix it means 'I will': which is fully stated in Hebrew as *ehyeh* *(aleph-hey-yod-hey)*. The full form is used of active engagement in Hebrew. [115] It is used of God's deeds pursuant to covenant; e.g. "I will be your God and you will be my people" (Jeremiah 7:23); "I will make of you a great nation" (Genesis 12:2). These 'I wills' are the active 'I' of God. The 'spare' *alephs* indicate this active 'I'.

In a core statement of His identity, in Exodus 3:14, the Lord introduces His name to Moses at the burning bush with the repeated word *ehyeh* and says (verse 15) "This is My Name forever". As noted in

---

[114] The Lubavitcher Rebbe, Menachem Schneerson, discusses the hidden nature of the *aleph* and how it alludes to Divine revelation in *A talk on Shabbos Parshas Emor, 5751.*

[115] Because of the construction of Hebrew, the root word *hyeh* is not used simply to refer to the existence of something or somebody. It is a "dynamic statement concerning the being of a person or thing" expressed through action towards others. Jenni, E., & Westermann, C. (1997). *Theological Lexicon of the Old Testament.* Peabody, Mass.; Hendrickson, p360.

the previous step, the use of the Hebrew word 'forever' alludes to hidden things. The 'spare' *alephs* of Genesis 1:1 point to His name and to His active but hidden presence.

Before stating His name to Moses, the Lord speaks in verse 12 of a sign that "I will be *(ehyeh)* with you". In step seven, we saw that the letters *aleph-tav* can mean both 'sign' and 'together with'. Thus the sign of Exodus 3:12 and the sign of the *aleph-tav* coincide and both refer to a sign of the closeness of God to us. Both chime with the words "God is with us" (Immanuel) in Isaiah 7:14, 8:8 and 8:10. The active 'will' of God is both His name and a sign of God with us. This God who is with us has been connected with the Messiah in Hebraic thought in these and other verses.[116]

Thus, the 'spare' *alephs* of Genesis 1 point to the hidden 'I wills' and identity of the Creator. They hint of the sign of God with us in the New Covenant, the *aleph-tav*. This hidden but active 'I' of God is with us from first to last through the son, *aleph*, of man and the son, *aleph*, of God. This is the covenant expression of *ehyeh*: the "I will be" of God. The *aleph* and the *ehyeh* are both forward looking: "I will". The picture is vivid and the story is not yet finished.

The letter *aleph* in the midst of 'son of man' and in the middle of 'son of God' is the active presence of God amid both, just as it is the presence of God amid the tree. The *aleph* stands between the first set of letters for *bar* (son) and the letters for *sheth*. It stands between the second set of letters for *bar* and the letters for *Elohim*. In both cases it connects them, suggesting that the son becomes the son of man by virtue of the *aleph* and the son becomes the son of God by virtue of the *aleph*.

The repeated *aleph* demonstrates the nature of the son and indicates that the two sons – son of man and son of God – are one and the same: the son who connects mankind to God and God to mankind. This explains why the *sheth* figure is appointed to the seat of judgement. The son who makes this two-fold connection is uniquely equipped to judge mankind on behalf of God.

The nature of the connection can be illustrated by looking at the letters between the two 'spare' *alephs*.

א שׁיתבר א

---

[116] For example, the *Talmud, Sukkah* 52a discusses the reference in Isaiah 7:14 in Messianic terms.

Going back to components (l) and (m), we can identify two words between the *alephs*:

שׁי *Shay* and תבר *Tebar*

This gives us a gift of homage *(shay)* that is broken in judgement *(tebar)*. Placed between the *alephs,* these words demonstrate that the connection shown by the two *alephs* is not shadow play or abstract symbolism. They point to a gift that is offered in homage and that is broken in judgement. A real gift, a real judgement, and a real victim are involved. As noted earlier, this configuration occurs between the first and second creation. It is located on God's time chart.

The double *ehyeh* introduced as the name of God in Exodus 3:14 is interspersed with the relative particle meaning 'who', 'which', 'what' or 'that'. Similarly, *shay* and *tebar* lie between the two *alephs*. The twin *ehyehs* and the twin *alephs* parallel each other. Accordingly, the *shay* and *tebar* may tell us who or what the active 'I' of God is in Exodus 3:14. They hint that this is the gift of homage broken in judgement. [117] If so, this lies at the core of the identity of the God of Israel.

We saw that the first two words in the Bible can be read as 'the son I appoint to creation'. There are two 'I's hinted at here: the 'I' who appoints and the son who is appointed. They are both present in the beginning and they are both singular. The *alephs* bring together the father who appoints and the son who is appointed, so that there is "God with us". The *alephs* may be no more than a breath but their action is powerful.

However, the active 'I' of God who says "I will" produces a time puzzle. If all that we have found lies in the beginning, then it precedes sin and the consequent need for sacrifice. Why the need for sacrifice? And, if the story is forward looking, where are we now on God's timeline?

The full working out of God's plan in the past, present and future is a mystery to time bound mortals. The reference to Sheth in the first word in the Bible takes us from the beginning of creation to the other side of the Garden of Eden and, indeed, to the other side of the first murder by Cain of Abel. It leads us to the consequent hope of a Messiah who will put things right. Before Eve called, the Lord had

---

[117] Similarly, the written form of *aleph* in the Proto-Sinaitic script is a bull's head. So, the twin *alephs* suggest the two bulls that were to be sacrificed at each new moon at the beginning of the lunar month.

answered her search. From the beginning, from the first word in the Bible, God had a plan for relationship and for resolving the separation between Creator and creation. The *Torah* was not a response to sin, but pre-existent as God's plan.[118]

God's covenant is not restricted to a moment in time or a particular generation. Moses, speaking to a later generation than those who received the Ten Commandments at Mount Horeb, says:

> The Lord our God made a covenant with us at Horeb. The Lord did not make this covenant with our fathers, but with us, with all of us alive here today. The Lord spoke to you face to face at the mountain from the midst of the fire...   (Deuteronomy 5:2–4)

For Moses, the Lord spoke face to face at Mount Horeb with a generation not yet born. Such a perspective has a timeline, but sees the making of covenant as both eternal and fresh to each generation: "The Lord did not make this covenant with our fathers, but with us, all of us alive here today."

The title 'son of God' follows the title 'son of man'. This is a clue that the nature of the son of man is revealed to creation before that of the son of God. The action or revelation of the son does not occur in one single moment. Our previous findings fit with this. There are two creations and a timeline connecting them.

Proceeding through the first four words of Genesis and bringing together what we have learned so far:

- we start from the first *bet* of creation in the beginning;

- this incorporates or leads to the son of man, in connection with the first *bara* (first act of creation) and the first *aleph* amid the first tree;

- we move through the breaking of a sacrifice as a result of judgement and the second *aleph*;

- we arrive at revelation of the son of God in connection with the second *bara* (second act of creation) and in connection with the second tree.

We move from the first to the last and to the final completion in the second creation. As with component (u) previously, we find that there first may be a partial completion, with a gap before the full disclosure

---

[118] *Talmud, Shabbat* **88b**.

of Messiah and the full completion of the Creator's plan. He is disclosed first as son of man and only later fully revealed as son of God. A gap between the appearances of the Messiah is also suggested in Judaic literature.[119] This is in the Divine plan from the beginning.

The *aleph* is both a sign of "God is with us" and part of the *aleph-tav*, the sign of the New Covenant. The New Covenant is both the first and the last. If the *aleph* is the sign of the first, it must also lead to the conclusion, to the sign of the last, the *tav*. It does this through the *beth*, that is to say, through the house of the Lord. This house cannot be restricted to the physical temple in Jerusalem, as that temple was only for a limited time. God is with us now in the house of the Lord. We need to find Him.

In step ten we will learn more of how the *alephs* resonate with the whole message of the first four words. First let us contrast this presence of the active 'I' of God with an absence in the opening words.

Component y: the absence

The *aleph* speaks of God's presence. The next clue speaks of an absence or lack of completion. Absence can be shown by the consistent absence of an expected letter. To look at such an absence is not adding something to the text or altering it. Instead, it is like, say, an expected note or beat in the rhythm that is omitted in a jazz piece. The absence becomes part of the tune and draws attention to itself for those who listen carefully. Silence speaks. As we have remarked, the omission of letters to the normal spelling of words in the Hebrew Bible is regarded as significant and worth analysis.

In this study we have come across the repeated absence of a letter. We have found six words which can be written with or without the letter *vav*, and which are written without the *vav* in Genesis 1:1:

y)   רוֹשׁ or רֹאשׁ *Rosh*   component (d)
                                        destitution

---

[119] *Ruth Rabbah* 5:6 says that after the first deliverer (Moses, who delivered Israel from Egypt), there will be a second (the Messiah) who will reveal himself and then withdraw for a while, just as Moses did. Later Judaic literature often sees Moses as the first Messiah, with a second Messianic figure coming afterwards. The idea of three stages with the Messiah – revelation, concealment and revelation – is widespread. See, for example, *Bamidbar Rabbah* 11 (12th C CE).

ברוש or ברש *Berosh*	component (k)	tree
תבור or תבר *Tebar*	component (m)	brokenness
אולם or אלם *Ulam*	component (q)	entrance to the temple
הוי or הי *Hoy*	component (r)	lament
אות or את *Owth*	component (u)	sign

In Hebrew, the letter *vav* serves as a linking word between others, and is used in the sense of 'and', 'or' and so forth. Symbolically it is seen primarily as indicating completion or continuity. In the opening phrase of Genesis, the *vavs* which stand for completion are missing. Hence, there is incompletion. This confirms the previous picture of incompleteness amongst the completion. The lack of continuity also suggested by the absent *vavs* may point to a series of discrete events in contrast to a smooth unfolding over time.

The *vav*, as the sixth letter of the alphabet, is associated with man because man was created on the sixth day in the creation account. The pattern of absent *vavs* suggests both the absence of humanity from whatever the arrangements or plan may be that are described by the entry code, yet the need for our presence to obtain completion.

Contrast the absence of the *vavs* in the six words listed above with the presence of the 'spare' *alephs*. The story of the opening phrase is woven by the presence of the *alephs* – symbolising the active 'I' of God or the connection between God and man – and not by the *vavs* symbolising the connection or completion stemming from man. The emphasis is on what God is doing rather than on what humanity is doing. If we look first to our own strength or action, then we will find incompleteness – the absent *vavs* – and miss the presence of the *alephs*, the active 'I' of God.

We saw under component (d) that, when the *aleph* replaces the silent letter *vav*, then the word meaning 'head' can also mean 'destitution'. That is, the head of the house of creation becomes destitute because *aleph* replaces *vav*. The presence of the active 'I' of God here leads to the destitution of His house. Similarly, under component (k), we saw that the word *berosh* (tree) can be spelt with or without a *vav* prior to the final *shin*. Again, *aleph* appears instead of *vav*, this time amid the tree. Through this *aleph*, the head becomes both the subject of destitution and is entangled with the tree. The active 'I' of God replaces our own action. The substitution of *aleph* for *vav* in the first word of Genesis 1:1 brings problems for the head of creation, the head of God's house. The *aleph* also sets fire to the tree.

Under component (u), a specific sign *(aleph-vav-tav)* is associated with each of the great statements of covenant in the *Tanach* except for the New Covenant. We argued that the *aleph-tav* points to the sign of the New Covenant. If so, that sign alone amongst the covenant signs lacks the *vav*. The hint is that this sign is less directly dependent upon human participation. Hence, this covenant and this sign can be hidden in the beginning before the appearance of the heavens or the earth or human beings. This covenant is somehow settled before their creation. Yet, there is incompletion precisely because of the absent *vav*.

We have spoken of that which is hidden in Genesis 1:1. This does not imply that such matters are inaccessible or remote. The letter *vav* is shaped like a hook and the Hebrew word *vav* (consisting of the letter *vav* repeated) means 'hook'. In the Bible it is used only of the hooks for the curtains around the courtyard of the tabernacle that separate the holy from the mundane and of the hooks for the veil guarding the entrance to the Ark of the Covenant. The word *vav* tells us of barriers to approaching the presence of God. The absence of *vavs* in Genesis 1:1 suggests the absence of such barriers and the direct accessibility of God. We are absent; He is accessible. This access must be through the *aleph*, the active 'I' of God.

The Hebrew words for 'sign', for 'lament', for 'entrance to the temple', for 'brokenness', for 'tree' and for 'destitution' lack their *vavs*. They are linked together by this incompletion. If the *aleph*, the active 'I' of God, is not recognised, then the sign, the lament, the entry to the temple, the brokenness, the tree, and the destitution of the head of the house all remain incomplete or they are not recognised. Their completion or fruitfulness rests on the presence of the *alephs*, not on the absent *vavs*. To grasp this is to see the presence of God in our story. To fail to grasp this is to fail to see God with us.

Elohim is 'together with' us, as we have seen. The Creator has stepped into His creation to provide completion, yet there is still incompletion. If there is only a partial completion, what will bring the conclusion?

The *vavs* bring completion and stand for our role in doing so: the connections we are to make based on our relationship with Him. Adam was given work to do and everything that was created still requires work by us.[120] So also does realisation of that 'together with' of *Elohim:* He together with us and us together with Him. Full completion awaits our response to the provision God has made on our behalf. That provision is through covenant sacrifice. The response is awaited from those who are in covenant relationship with the Creator. This can provide the basis for *tikkun olam:* the repair of the universe. That is why the second *aleph-tav* of Genesis 1:1 links the heavens and the earth through the presence of the *vav.* We are needed.

The *aleph-tav* sign of the New Covenant lacks the *vav.* By contrast, the sign of the Abrahamic covenant and the sign of the Mosaic covenant both include the *vav.* The *vavs* in these cases refer to the role of Israel; Israel is peculiarly God's vehicle through these two covenants. The missing *vav* in the sign of the`1 New Covenant, which is with Israel, may also refer to Israel, but in this case Israel is missing. Something is awaited from her to bring completion.

In Hebrew the letter *vav* can fulfil the function of inverting the tense of a verse: from past to future or future to past. The first such usage occurs in verse three of Genesis: "And God said... ". The *vav* here inverts the verb from future to past tense, so that it becomes "God said". The absence of *vavs* in the opening words of Genesis shows that there is no such inversion occurring there. One could say that the account is given from the Lord's viewpoint, without that confusion over time that arises with the human perspective.

From our own human and time bound viewpoint, we can begin to make sense of this account. To return to the history sketched in the previous component, a new part can be added, the fourth in this list:

- we start from the first *bet* of creation in the beginning,

- this incorporates or leads to the son of man, in connection with the first *bara* (first act of creation) and the first *aleph* amid the first tree;

- we move through the breaking of a sacrifice as a result of judgement and the second *aleph*;

---

[120] *Beresheith Rabbah* 11:6.

- we await the response of those in covenant relationship with God, in particular Israel, to the active 'I' of God and the covenant sacrifice; when that sacrifice is accepted, then

- we arrive at revelation of the son of God in connection with the second *bara* (second act of creation) and in connection with the second tree.

There is a veiled suggestion in the absent *vavs* and spare *alephs* that the second and third stages will be missed by many. The action of the Messiah will not be recognised. The result is a partial completion and the need to await completion.

The absent *vavs* remind us of an aching absence in God's scheme under the Mosaic covenant. There is no temple, no priesthood and no offering for sin and has been none since 70 CE when the temple in Jerusalem was destroyed. Since then, the Mosaic covenant as specified in the *Torah* necessarily lacks completion. The absent *vavs* direct us to the answer to this absence and this incompletion. There is a covenant sacrifice in the temple of creation that marks completion, and it has been planned from the beginning. Here is where God's presence is found; here is where He calls us to completeness.

Summary: the barest breath

Two strands are threaded through the beginning. Together they bring out the underlying message of the entry code.

The spare *alephs* provide a signature running through the opening word and direct attention towards the son figure. The son of man and son of God are one: the son who connects man to God and God to man, the realization of the active 'I' of God. The twin *alephs* parallel the name that God introduces Himself to Moses with in Exodus 3:14. They help us understand the hidden but active 'I' of God and the sign of God with us. They identify this active 'I' with a gift of homage broken in judgement. This may lie at the core of God's identity.

The son of man is in the beginning and is head of the house of the Lord, the house of creation. The son has yet fully to be revealed to creation as the son of God. When He is, that will bring the final *tav*, the conclusion to creation, and will see the realisation of all the promises in the Bible. This will be the new creation, the second *barah* of Genesis 1:1 and the final revelation of the son of God.

God is present in and from the beginning. His action, through the son, has not been fully revealed. Given the disasters and suffering of the current world, He may appear absent to us. This leads to the uncertainties or dualities we have come across: creation is associated with being cut down, the head is associated with destitution; the priest is heir to corruption, the judge is associated with shame and the *aleph* amid the tree points to a gift of homage or to corruption.

The active 'I' of God takes on our burden to His cost. God is not absent from our story but His action is hidden. The conclusion and unveiling are still to come. They rest on our response, in particular Israel's response, to the active 'I' of God. Collectively, humanity is the thread that is absent. Our absence is replaced by His presence.

In combination, the *alephs* and the *yods* provide a strange dynamic: we are replaced so that relationship can be established and maintained, yet our presence is sought and is necessary for that relationship.

Step nine shows us that, when we recognise the active 'I' of God, then we can act in partnership with Him, then there can be completion, then what is priestly will be clearly distinguished from what is corrupt, what is a gift of homage from corruption. Then the head of God's house will be recognised and separated from destitution and shame. Then the heavens and the earth are joined with their Creator. Then "the earth will be filled with the glory of the Lord, as the waters cover the sea." (Habakkuk 2:14).

"Here I Am"
Assembling the Message

A preliminary overview and test of what we have found

T he *Tanach* tells us that now is the day not only to seek Him but to find Him:

> Those who rule over them howl, and My name is continually blasphemed all day long. Therefore, My people shall know My name; therefore, in that day I am the one who is speaking, "Here I am".
> (Isaiah 52:5–6)

In that day we are told to look for Him and to know Him in His Name. "That day" speaks of painful times, even the birth pangs of Messiah.[121] We have looked for Him in the beginning and found that *Elohim* both cries with woe – the *oy* of God – and says "Here I am". Perhaps we are in "that day" when we can find Him.

Through nine steps we have explored the first four words in the Bible, digging deep to extract as much as possible of the information they contain. The enquiry has been painstaking, treating each

---

[121] The characteristics of the birth pangs of Messiah, *Chevlei Mashiach*, are discussed in *Talmud, Sanhedrin* 98a–b *Beresheith Rabbah* 42:4 and *Pesikta Rabbati* 37:2

component as part of God's first and most urgent communication. We have looked at:

- the first verse as a whole in step one

- individual components within each of the first four words in steps one to seven

- ways of reading these in combination in step eight

- the patterns of letters that run through the first four words in step nine, and also in step ten which lies ahead.

We have seen how the various clues and hints direct our study toward passages in the Bible where the same words or concepts occur. In turn, these passages illuminate the opening words. We have found intricacy and seen how the many clues cross-refer and interlock with each other and the wider Bible.

God is revealed even in the tiniest detail of Scripture. We have found in these details a burning house, family, heartbreak, a sign, hidden names, and mysterious patterns of letters. In this chapter we shall briefly survey the twenty-five components discussed so far and consider how they fit together and what emerges from this. The results will provide the material for stating the entry code.

The main points

Let us review our findings so far and see if they will reveal to us the "here I am" of God. Here is a list of the main points (the letters in brackets are those used to identify the different components in the preceding discussion):

Step one: the act of creation

- The distinction between Creator and creation poses the problem of relationship between the two. (a)
- The Creator becomes knowable to us through His act of creation and through engagement with His creation. Creation, the house of the Creator, is open. (a)
- Creation is in the beginning and humanity is the peak of creation and created in God's image. This gives us responsibility in His creation. (b)

- To discover more we should read the book, beginning at the beginning. (a)

Step two: the burning house

- Wisdom, the word of God, is there in the beginning. The beginning points to first fruits and to the need for fruitfulness. (c)
- The beginning also points to the need for sacrifice in order to provide a basis for new beginnings and restoration. Creation may be destroyed. (c)
- There is a head – His head – in the house in the beginning. The head is associated with destitution. (d)
- The house is the temple of God and the head is its cornerstone. (d), (e)
- Covenant is in the beginning and is the basis of establishing relationship, linking Creator and creation through blood sacrifice. (f)
- The covenant is His foundation. Without covenant, we face the consuming fire of God. (g)

Step three: family

- A son is in the beginning and in creation but precedes them both and has primacy. This son is head of the house. 'Son' is the first repeated word in the Bible. (h)
- This son is associated with purity or purification, with a grain of wheat and thus with the word of God, and with sacrifice. (h)
- The figure of *sheth* is in the beginning. He is the appointed one and represents Eve's Messianic hope, expressed in the name of her son Sheth, the ancestor of all humanity. He is associated with shame and with the good gone bad. (i)
- The *sheth* figure is central to creation and may sit in judgement. (j)

Step four: broken connections

- A tree is in the beginning. However, completion is lacking. (k)
- The head is amid the tree. The symbol for the link between God and man is amid the tree and sets it and its fruit aflame. (k)
- This symbol connects the son with a gift of homage from creation to the Creator. (l)
- The tree is connected with the sign for both divine power and for corruption. (l)

- The tree leads to the end or conclusion of covenant. The end is found in the beginning. It is associated with a judgement that breaks or destroys. A gift is broken in sacrifice there. (m)
- The first word in the Bible also provides the title of the book. The components of the word *beresheith* are the components of the title of the first book of the *Torah*. (b) – (m)

Step five: the arrow

- The term 'creation' is used in specific ways of God's action. He is ongoingly but selectively involved in creative power with Israel and with those who seek Him. This is because we need Him. (n)
- Two creations are hinted at: the first is earthly; in the second the Divine is more directly revealed. Sitting in the place of judgement, the *sheth* figure may lie between the two creations. (n)

Step six: the Creator's heartbreak

- The word for God hints at the possibility of a unified God. (o)
- His name is identified with a covenant oath and the consequences of breaking it. (p)
- This hint also points to a strong tree which is a place of both danger and of hope. This tree is connected to God's perspective, whilst the previous tree is connected to mankind's perspective. (p)
- This covenant oath or this tree are hidden and associated with Messiah. (r)
- The word for God contains the root word for a sheaf of wheat bound in sacrifice or a person bound in silence. This is the basis of entry into God's temple, into His presence. (q)
- God exclaims in woe from amid the sheaf of wheat. The sacrifice hurts God. (r)
- *Elohim* is the Lord whose suffering is hidden, the one who cries out from amid the sacrifice. (s)

Step seven: the sign

- *Elohim* is associated with the first and the last, which is both in the beginning and is also completion. The wholeness of God's plan encompasses all of creation for all time. (t)
- This first and last is a sign of covenant and marks a partial completion. It is the missing sign of the New Covenant, an everlasting covenant. The New Covenant is the covenant of the

beginning and the end. This sign and this covenant are inherently 'together with': that is they rest on, or lead to, cooperation between God and humanity. (u)

Step eight: hidden names

- The first four words hide the name: 'The son I appoint to creation (or to creating), the first and last'. This son is the mediator between God and creation appointed in the beginning. (v)
- The first four words hide the name: 'Son, son of man, son of God, the first and the last'. The title is Messianic and is linked to the firstborn or first fruits. This son precedes and encompasses creation. (w)
- The son of man succeeds both the priestly Abel and the corrupt Cain. He is both priest and offering. The son of God is perfect. The son of man may be revealed before the son of God. Completion lies in the future. (w)
- The son of man, son of God, as Messiah stands in the gap for all humanity and provides the sacrifice necessary for the New Covenant. He is the first fruits, the head that becomes desolate, the fruit of the tree burnt in the fire, the appointed one subject to shame, the gift of homage broken in judgement and the sheaf of wheat that is the price of entry to the temple and which causes God woe. (c), (d), (h), (i), (k), (m), (q), (r)

Step nine: the barest breath

- The *aleph* symbolises the connection between God and man, the active 'I' of God engaged with His creation, the barest breath of the knowledge of God. The *aleph* links the Messiah figure, the son of man and son of God, to a gift of homage broken in judgement. (x)
- The two 'spare' *alephs* of Genesis 1:1 parallel the name of God introduced at the burning bush in Exodus 3:14. They help us understand the hidden but active 'I' of God and the sign of God with us. They identify this active 'I' with a gift of homage broken in sacrifice. (x)
- If we look to our own strength, there will be incompleteness and we will miss the 'I' of God. But completion, the repair of the universe and the harmony of creation, awaits our response. (y)
- A possible history can be constructed:
  - we start from creation in the beginning,

- this incorporates or leads to the son of man, in connection
  with the first *bara* (first act of creation) and the first *aleph* amid
  the first tree,
- we move through the breaking of a sacrifice as a result of
  judgement and the second *aleph*,
- we await the response of those in covenant relationship with
  God, in particular Israel, to the active 'I' of God and the
  covenant sacrifice; when that sacrifice is accepted, then
- we arrive at revelation of the son of God in connection with
  the second *bara* (second act of creation) and in connection with
  the second tree. (m), (t), (x), (y)

"Here I am"

As remarked in the opening chapter, the Creator of life evidently knows
how to compress, transfer and secure vital information. If we look
within the Hebrew and let it speak to us, we can hear Him speaking:
"Keep silent and let Me speak... Keep silent and I will teach you
wisdom" (Job 33:31 and 33). The Lord is giving us a location, saying
"Here I am." For example, the four name or titles of God we have
found provide quite a precise description. We should be able to find
Him.

The Lord tells us to listen and declares that He both conceals and
reveals:

> Listen, O my people to my teaching; incline your ear to
> the words of my mouth. I will open my mouth in a
> parable; I will utter dark sayings [riddles] of old, which
> we have heard and known, and our fathers have told us.
> We will not conceal them from their children...
> (Psalm 78:1–4a)

We have listened to what the opening words say. The thirty-nine
points listed above provide a detailed and precise picture. This is no
mere assemblage of assorted bits and pieces, glued together in some
sort of order of our own imagining. What we have found is far from
random. The enquiry is uncovering a coherent structure, the
foundation for a greater whole: "precept upon precept". Simply
reading through the list of points demonstrates this. As the pieces of
the code are assembled, they articulate a message to us. That message
reads like a rehearsal of the major subjects running through the *Tanach*.

Before the description of creation week in the first chapter of Genesis the first verse specifies the relationship between Creator and creation. The divide between Creator and creation is the harsh challenge set out there. The response is provided by the components uncovered within the same verse. The topics and ideas they present build piece by piece and interlock in clusters. The points join up to form a picture. There are complexities and repetitions but every piece fits and adds to the composition. The combined whole resonates with a strong message.

That message states both God's sovereign reign and authority over creation and His engagement with it. The countervailing themes are inescapable. As the *Tanach* says: "His glory is above earth and heaven" (Psalm 148:13), yet "the whole earth is full of His glory" (Numbers 14:21, Psalm 72:19, Isaiah 6:3). To put it another way, the components we have discussed bring out both the transcendence of the Almighty as Creator and Lord of all and His imminence to us as He is actively engaged with His creation. Both aspects are found at the beginning of the Bible, as well as the time dimension in which this dynamic is worked out. He provides a bridge across the divide so that we can participate in His plan for history and there can be 'together with'. He expresses His loving kindness and calls to us in mercy. Yet there is the gulf between Creator and creation and there is judgement.

From our side, the tension remains between love and fear of the Lord: He is Lord; we are family. Again, a duality seems to operate. Our participation in God's plan is invited and needed for completion, yet the basis of that plan is to replace our action with His. We can see the broad framework but the dynamics occurring within it are not yet clear, in particular the nature of our role.

In the opening chapter, three levels of discussion were distinguished: pursuing the detail of the text and the hints it gives; assembling the consequent points to obtain a wider view, and gaining understanding and application of the message that is revealed. With this chapter, we now have an overview of the findings from this enquiry and discussion at the first two levels is near complete. But the meaning and application of the message that emerges remains rather opaque.

This leads to a challenge. What exactly does He want from us to bring the kingdom of heaven to fruition; how can we mend or end the incompletion we have found? We should expect the entry code to complete the discussion and equip us to answer.

That so much – thirty nine points to summarise what we have found so far – should emerge from examining just four words is testimony to the power of the *Tanach*. But, how can the reader have confidence in these findings and the direction in which they lead?

Reasons for confidence

Before proceeding to address the challenge of what He wants from us, let us reconsider our starting point. We set out five reasons for confidence in our method in the first chapter of this enquiry. Three of these related to the nature of our discourse based in Hebrew and the extreme tightness of our focus. We have observed these and remained anchored in Hebrew Scripture and study. One reason related to the four different approaches to be adopted and which have duly been employed. The fifth reason was the tests to be imposed on the findings.

Let us briefly apply these tests:

- *Inclusive:* Remaining within the limits of our discourse and the strict criteria for inclusion (stated in the opening chapters of this enquiry), our discussion has included every hint that we can find in the first four Hebrew words of Genesis. None have been excluded. Because coverage is total, this enquiry has taken nine steps (with a tenth to come) to cover only four Hebrew words.

- *Precise:* The thirty-nine points appear to be consistent and to fit together precisely. The closer we look the more exactly the pieces fit with each other.

- *Coherent:* The final picture will emerge in the following chapters, but we can see the points cohere together to tell a meaningful story concerning how to bridge the gulf between the Creator and creation.

- *Robust:* The components reinforce each other and, for example, the concepts emerging from the first word, *Beresheith,* also emerge from the third word, *Elohim.* Several components could be removed and the overall argument would still emerge, albeit with reduced clarity. Consistency and duplication give it robustness and make the message hard to evade.

- *Appropriate:* The composition emerging is entirely appropriate to its location at the head of the Bible. It addresses the issue produced by the opening statement in Genesis and whose resolution is threaded throughout the *Tanach*.

- *Powerful:* As it unfolds, the message illuminates the deepest themes in the Bible and unlocks our understanding of Scripture. It is not about an adjunct or secondary matter.

- *Relevant:* The entry code is no theological stance or goal statement. It concerns real issues which address our deepest needs. However, the precise articulation and application remain to be seen.

- *Elegant:* At this point, our findings have not yet clearly fulfilled this test. Complexity has yet to be reduced to an essential simplicity.

- *Connected (to actual events):* This has not been covered.

- *Unique:* This is an open invitation to the reader. Can the reader find some other way of assembling the findings from this enquiry that is:

  - meaningful

  - complies with the nature of the discourse

  - meets the rules that we have applied, and

  - passes the other tests listed above?

Applying these ten tests, a strong case can be made that our findings fulfil six of them. The results of the enquiry so far are: inclusive, fit together precisely, and are coherent, robust, appropriate, and powerful. Four tests remain to be convincingly and fully met: relevance, elegance, being connected, and uniqueness. Judgement is suspended, but we know the characteristics that the final articulation of the entry code must fulfil.

We have brought the different components together to look at them in combination and check the results. As in an archaeological excavation, the components come in a given sequence provided by the Hebrew text of Genesis, with some nested inside each other. The pieces fit together into a coherent configuration. Through nine steps, we have considered twenty-five components that can be decoded through careful examination of the opening words. Some of the components are multi-faceted. Together, they yield the points listed above.   In combination, these show an intricate, inter-related and powerful set of ideas. But the picture is not yet complete.

The meaning comes pouring out of the opening words, demonstrating the richness of the *Tanach* and the power of its words. To avoid being overwhelmed by what we have found, let us catch our breath. The next step provides an aid to contemplation. It is the last of the ten steps of this enquiry before the entry code is specified and its implications drawn out and considered.

Though the music is complex, the rhythm is constant. The words of Genesis 1:1 speak to us of what most needs to be said, and speak prophetically of all that is and is to come. We must cast our own preconceptions aside if we are to hear God and align ourselves with His heartbeat. So, let us turn to what is His.

Step 10: Recovering the question

A final component that tells of the hand of the Creator, of His image and of finding our identity there.

C an we know the character of the Creator? Through this we would become able to speak about, think about, and engage with Him. If we seek Him and He seeks us, such a meeting is the fulfilment of His plan for us.

The previous chapter brought together the components of this enquiry to locate the "here I am" of God. We have a picture of His location and how He deals with creation. How can we make this alive to us? Step ten considers the smallest letter in the Hebrew alphabet, the letter *yod*, as an aid to contemplation. It will throw light on what we have found so that we can ponder the implications. The *yod* will show us how to know what is uniquely His and what He shares with us. This is not an impossible step and it does not require the suspension of disbelief. Rather it invites the engagement of our reason.

This enquiry began by considering the first verse as a whole, and then looked at individual components within the first four words. We then considered ways of reading these in combination. Step nine examined patterns of letters that run through the four words. Each of these four levels illuminates and provides a cross-check on the others.

Step nine drew out the significance of the absent *vavs*. In step ten, this is contrasted with the recurring presence of the letter *yod* in the first four words. In Hebrew the *vav*, is used as the third person possessive (that is, what belongs to somebody else) and the *yod* is used to mark the first person possessive (that is, what belongs to the speaker). The first four words of Genesis focus on the first person possessive (what is 'mine') not the third person possessive (what is 'his'). As these words speak of God, they focus on what belongs to God rather than what belongs to us. The entry code is stated in terms of the active 'I' of God and what is 'mine', that is what belongs to God. This is the message of the repeated *aleph* of step nine and the repeated *yod* discussed here. The more distant, third person 'his' and the association with man through the letter *vav* does not occur. This is a personal statement by God about His actions. Genesis 1:1 both sets out God's act of creating and His actions and purpose in creation.

This can help with a deep enigma. Genesis 1:26-27 states that man (*adam*) is made and created in God's image.[122] This crucial statement tells us that we are the pinnacle of God's creation. "The love of God for humans is manifested in the act that God created them in His image, and especially, that He revealed this to them".[123] These verses see the first appearance of the term *adam* and the first appearance of the possessive (both 'our' and 'his') in the plain text of the Bible. It is the first time God speaks of Himself and He does so in terms of us being in the Creator's image.

If we are in the Creator's image then we are a representation or likeness of Him. These verses imply that there is an image of God for us to seek and find and refer to and that this is central to who we are. But where is the reference point to show us He whom we are like and are to represent, and thus to show us how we are to act? If we are to relate closely to somebody or use them as a model, we need to know them. A contract, even a covenant, is insufficient.

In Genesis 5:3 Adam refers to Sheth as "in his own likeness, according to his image". This is the next time after Genesis 1:27 that such a turn of phrase is used. In the language of the Bible, to be in someone's "image and likeness" means to be that person's child. It is not a matter of having some characteristic in common. Nor is it a matter of possession. Rather, it is an all-encompassing statement, a matter of relationship: of the blood and of the heart. Sheth is the son of Adam and we are sons of God. To be in God's image entails having

---

[122] The switch from plural to singular and from "make" to "create" between verse 26 and verse 27 has occasioned discussion but is beyond our scope here.
[123] *Talmud, Pirkei Avoth* 3:18.

a close bond with Him.[124] Anything less is to deny who we are, just as a son who denies his father denies his own identity.

How are we to know the Father or relate to Him? There is no evident image of God mentioned in the text prior to Genesis 1:26–27. Can we be intended to refer to the Creator moving in creative power? This seems too difficult, the gulf too great. The name *Elohim*, used in Genesis 1:1, is primarily used in the *Tanach* for God acting as the God of judgement. This is far from us. Later the Bible forbids the making and worshipping of any idol or likeness (Exodus 20:4–5). The fire in the temple was the symbol of the presence of God. If we try to handle such fire for ourselves we risk the same fate as the sons of Aaron who were destroyed for that. The Ark of the Covenant – the focus for God's presence in the Jerusalem temple – was hidden from human sight in the Holy of Holies. The only exception was the visit by the high priest once a year on the Day of Atonement.

We are instructed to be holy for the Lord is holy (Leviticus 11:44; 11:45; 19:2; 20:7) but we lack an immediate image of what the holiness of God is. We are told to cleave to and to walk after the Lord (Deuteronomy 13:4) but His distance and His fire seem to be barriers to this.[125] God given laws and discipline can provide a path toward God[126] but they are not themselves His image: we can 'walk after' Him, but still do not know His image. The 'together with' is lacking.

As we are created in His image and are sons of God, can we study and promote ourselves as a reference point and to promote God's plan for the world? This is tempting but dangerous. Step one spoke of the gulf between Creator and creation. If we look to ourselves to bridge this, we will tend to make Him in our flawed image and start to see ourselves as like gods on the basis of our own merits. We end up loving ourselves and attending to our own heartbeat. This is no trivial flaw: "You shall have no other gods before Me." (Exodus 20:3)

To be told that we are made in His image is to call us into relationship beyond ourselves. We must look beyond ourselves to

---

[124] Nosson Zvi Finkel (1849–1927, Lithuania and Russia) argues that it is the responsibility of every human being to act in such a way that he reflects favourably upon God whose image he bears and that every human being is created with the ability to live up to this.

[125] *Talmud Sotah* 14a asks how is it possible to cleave to God, and walk in His way, since He is described as a consuming fire. It explains that we must strive to cleave to the Divine Attributes and walk in His ways. *Talmud, Sanhedrin* 64a sees the passage from Deuteronomy as an instruction to keep in close contact with the Divine.

[126] *Rabbah Vayikrah* 25:3.

discover His image. A vague identity or concept of the Divinity is too easily shaped by our own thinking and to our own convenience.

Seemingly, we are left without any accessible image of God to refer to, other than ourselves. This elusiveness has led to the view that the highest level of knowledge, the knowledge of God, is not yet accessible to mankind. Nevertheless, some Judaic thought allows the barest breath of the knowledge of God to be transmitted to us.[127] We have seen this barest breath in the 'spare' *alephs* of component (x).

The components considered in this enquiry provide many specific details. The "Here I am" of God in the previous chapter is precise, not vague. Does the beginning of the Bible reveal the image of God?

Component z: the *yods*

The *yods* in the opening of Genesis provide a hint for they identify what particularly belongs to God. Within the text of the first verse, they yield: 'my head', 'my fire', 'my foundation', 'my tree', and 'my oath':

ראשי	'my head' component (d)
אשי	'my fire', or 'my foundation' component (g)
ברשי	'my tree' component (k)
אלהי	'my oath', 'my consequences of breaking an oath', or 'my strong tree' component (p) [128]

The speaker here in the beginning can only be the Creator. The four 'my's' are necessarily His. The head, the fire, the foundation, the tree, and the oath are all described as 'my'': that is, they are the Lord's.

The *alephs* of component (x) showed the active 'I' of God. The *yods* show us a different dimension. The first reveals the active and the

---

[127] That the highest gate of knowledge (of Torah) is not yet accessible to man is implied by Moses' failure to achieve it whilst alive (*Talmud, Rosh Hashanah* 21b and *Nedarim* 38a). The Vilna Gaon, Chiddushei HaRim (Poland 1798–1866) and others suggest that a slight knowledge at this highest level is possible or may be granted to those who pursue it.

[128] Strictly speaking, in Hebrew, when a word that ends with a ה becomes "my", "his", etc. then the ה usually becomes a ת.

second the possessive aspect of His presence in creation. We have discussed the active 'I' of His presence and found surprises. The possessive aspect of His presence also provides the unexpected.

Yod is the seminal letter of the Hebrew alphabet. It is the smallest and humblest of letters, yet from it the other letters originate. It cannot be divided into component parts, as the other letters can. The *yod* signifies the oneness or unity of *Elohim*. As mentioned earlier, the *yod* on its own represents the metaphysical, or hope in the life to come. Here, in the first verse, it may represent the nature of hope for creation.

Where is the Creator most strongly present, what is most His in all that we can see or find or conceive? What looks beyond our own circumstances and limitations yet speaks to our relationship with the Lord in the midst of these? The *yods* show us the answer. His head, His fire, His foundation, His tree, and His oath are peculiarly His. They point us to a more permanent holy place than the physical temple in Jerusalem or the Ark of the Covenant. The four *yods* set out in the beginning point us toward the image of God. They show His character towards us. We are to look for the head of His house who undergoes the covenant fire and fulfils the covenant oath in order to provide our foundation. This is through a tree.

The *yods* demonstrate a Creator who fulfils our side of the covenant through what is His. Our relationship with Him has its foundation provided through the covenant by means of His head, His tree, and His oath. Because of these, we can be spared the consuming fire of God, His fire. Malachi 4:1 warns of "the day that is coming, burning like a furnace". That is not an image of God we can bear.[129] The covenant sacrifice takes that fire in our stead.

The word *yod* itself – written *yod-dalet* – means 'hand'. So, these *yods* reveal the hand of God extended toward us. This is the hand that is first and last, that founded the earth and spread out the heavens (Isaiah 48:12–13), the loving kindness that is from everlasting to everlasting (Psalm 103:17). Genesis 1:1 makes known the hand of the Creator from first to last.

Deuteronomy 13:5, as other passages, instructs us to follow Him and to cling to Him. The *yods* show us more of Him so that we may better be able to follow and to cling to Him. These *yods* speak before "His image" is mentioned in Genesis 1:27. They provide the prior,

---

[129] Judaism is concerned to avert "the harsh decree" of God's judgement; see *Talmud, Shabbat* 119b and the *Unetaneh Tokef* prayer (originated c11th Century CE) for *Yom Kippur*.

indeed the first, delineation of what His character is like. Perhaps they
can disclose who or what is great enough to provide the image of the
Creator God to us, yet so tangible that we can grasp that image.

This leads to two problems. First, the forms we have discussed
seem inaccessible if they are to furnish His tangible image to us. These
words that are His seem remote (His head), or mysterious (His tree) or
too difficult to approach (His oath, His fire or His foundation). How
do they help us in practical terms to grasp His hand? Second, is there
any distinction between these words that are peculiarly His and the
other words within Genesis 1:1 that do not have the *yod* as a suffix? If
there is no clear distinction, then the discussion is only conjecture.

In using the *yods* as an aid to contemplation, we have gained a
fresh perspective on the findings that were brought together in the last
chapter. We can apply those findings to address the two problems just
raised, taking the second one first.

The head, the fire, the foundation, the tree and the oath have the
yod suffix. Within the first four words – and excluding those opening
words themselves – the following nouns do not have the *yod* as suffix:

creation	component (b)
house	component (e)
covenant	component (f)
son, or grain of wheat	component (h)
sheth, appointed one, shamefulness	component (i)
gift	component (l)
brokenness	component (m)
sheaf of wheat, entry to the temple	component (q)
lamentation	component (r)

Lacking the *yod* suffix, these words are not identified as specifically His. [130]

At first glance, this looks wrong. Surely the creation and the
house and the son are His since they belong to Him? In particular, if
the son is 'His son' why is there no *yod* as a suffix to it?

A distinction can be drawn between the two groups of words.
Those with the *yod* suffix belong to Him and solely to Him; they are His

---

[130] Both the word for gift of homage and for lamentation end with a *yod* as part of
their ordinary spelling. An additional *yod* would be necessary to identify the
masculine possessive.

possession alone and in no sense can we claim them. This includes 'His head' – a Divine not democratic appointment and 'His foundation' – which we can build on but cannot claim as our possession. Proverbs 10:25 speaks of a righteous one who is an eternal foundation, and Isaiah 28:16 of a foundation, a costly cornerstone, laid in Zion (Israel).[131] God has built the foundation. To think that we posses overall headship or that we can determine or build our own foundation is the beginning of error. If we appropriate His fire as our own, then either we may be consumed or others will be: the purging of heretics and non-believers in the name of God will begin and the auto-da-fe beckons. Such matters are not for us. The *yods* are His, not ours.

By contrast, creation, the house and the covenant are shared with us and we have responsibilities in respect of each of them. The entry to the temple is provided for us to use so as to draw close to Him. We are entitled to do so only because of the gift of homage, the sheaf of wheat, given as an offering from us to the Creator. But the offering comes from Him, provided on our behalf. Here is the gift that is broken in sacrifice. The lamentation and brokenness become ours as we come to understand the nature and the cost of that gift and weep with Him, as described in Zechariah 12:10. The appointed one – the *sheth* figure – may be in the seat of judgement upon creation but he is ours, our Messiah, rather than a remote and unapproachable judge.

What of the son figure? The son is His son but not reserved to Him for he is the son of man as well as the son of God. The son is His but also becomes ours, provided to us by God; the Messiah who stands in the gap on our behalf.

Hence, there is a distinction between the two sets of words. Those with the *yod* suffix are what the Creator holds to Himself and does not share with us; those without the suffix are shared with us. This distinction points to a Divine dynamic and underlines that an exchange or substitution lies at the heart of creation.

The two sets of words delineate that exchange. The oath and consequences of breaking that oath are described as 'my': they have become the Lord's although they arise from our side of the covenant. God takes on the consequences of our failure to fulfil covenant. Amazingly, the bad stuff becomes His. At the same time, the son of God does not remain exclusively His, but is shared with us as son of

---

[131] Proverbs 10:25 is in the singular, but has also been identified with righteous ones (plural) who may lead toward the Messiah, e.g. by Maimonides and the Vilna Gaon. Rashi and others identify the cornerstone of Isaiah 28:16 as the Messiah.

man. Righteousness belongs to Messiah, lack of righteousness to us but that righteousness is made available to us, as our lack is taken away and becomes His in our stead. He provides or shares good things with us and in return receives our failure. Our shameful clothing is taken away and replaced (Zechariah 3:3–4).

God, as the perfect giver, both gives and requires a perfect gift. This is achieved through our offering a gift of homage to Him: a gift received from Him in the first place. Instead of fire, we are provided with: a covenant that is fulfilled, a gift to offer so as to gain entry to the temple of His presence, and a house of creation that is shared.

The covenant sacrifice that He has placed in the temple on our behalf receives His consuming fire in our stead and gives us entry into His presence. An earlier chapter spoke of how the house of creation may appear to be on fire, yet still has a master. We can now see that he has taken that fire, that destruction, on himself in order to fulfil covenant. In this way, God's holiness is not compromised by His bonds with us. Yet, that holiness is made accessible to us, so that we can reflect it out into the world.

Genesis 1:1 shows us the foundation He has provided and its cost through its four 'my' words which specify what is His. How can we build on this so as to recognise the image in which we are made; how may we express godliness? The words of Genesis 1:1 that lack the *yod* give us the answer. They show us how we can approach God in His temple through what He shares with us. They tell us how we may grasp the *yod*, the hand of God extended towards us.

The actions of the Messiah on our behalf provide an image of God that we can take hold of. We can know the Father through the son. In the same way that the son is integral to creation, he is integral to our fulfilling our place in creation. He is our judge – the *sheth* figure – but a judge who is dedicated to help rather than to condemn.

But the exchange is not free; there is a cost to all this. The brokenness and the lamentation also lack the *yod* as suffix. They are not exclusively His. This tells us that we need to recognise and share the pain of the loss along with the benefits that it yields for us. If we are to join with Him, we need to recognise the exchange that has been made; to lament with Him and acknowledge our brokenness and shame in the cost of His sacrifice on our behalf. We have responsibilities too.

A stark warning lies in the *yods*. If we do not know what is His, then we lose the wisdom to recognise God's righteousness and holiness, the ability to hear His cry. We are called to know Him in order to know who we are ourselves; to know what is in His image and what is not. To be in somebody's image, a member of their family, is not the same as having their role or their strength. We need to be able to distinguish what is His, what is ours and what is shared. Then we can cooperate with Him and fulfil our role within the covenant relationship so that there can be 'together with'. Otherwise, the Divine image becomes tarnished; we no longer have clear direction and begin to lose knowledge of who we are. We may come to trust in our own actions rather than in His guidance and plan for us. The sacrifice of the Messiah becomes distorted, the covenant is undermined, the ability to love God dwindles, the bonds with Him are lost, corruption threatens, and disharmony reigns.

One could say that all religious error stems from taking one of the four *yod* words not as belonging to Him but as belonging to us: imaging that we own or can control or can become His head, fire, foundation, tree or oath. Such a move breaks the partnership between the Creator and ourselves and the Divine image becomes sullied. If we attempt to mend or unify creation not on His basis but on ours, then we lose our perspective and identity, lack foundation, and fail to represent Him. Where our actions are inappropriate, they can make the active 'I' of God hard to see. The curtain of the *vavs* is drawn across His presence and the *alephs* become difficult to identify.

Summary: recovering the question

We are made in the Creator's image. Revelation of Him into creation depends on us, on our ability to present and express His character in the world. To do so, we need to know that character. We have recovered the question.

In this step, we have used the *yods* to contemplate the message of first four words. We begin to see He in whose image we are made, so that we may cling to Him and know His character.

The last three components of this enquiry – the *alephs*, the *vavs*, and the *yods* – draw together its two core themes: the divide between Creator and creation, and the bridge provided across that gulf by the Creator in order to provide relationship:

- The *yods* show us what is His and that, through this, God maintains relationship with us by a Divine exchange. They show us His image and direct us to the hand of God.

- The *alephs* represent the active 'I' of God undertaking this in a hidden way, giving us the barest breath of the knowledge of God.

- The absence of the *vavs* shows that this is in place of what should be our responsibility and that the final completion awaits our response, in particular the response of Israel, so that the 'together with' of *Elohim* may be fully realised.

The *yods* illustrate the Creator taking on our burden and His hand extended towards us. The missing *vavs* and the spare *alephs* mark the Creator acting on our behalf and engaging with us. Together these three series of letters show how we may know Him in whose image we are made. They also locate His action in time: the hand of God is active from the beginning, the active 'I' of God has been undertaking the Divine dynamic, and the exchange has been made.

Something from us is awaited. The gulf between Creator and creation is resolved by the Creator taking on our part in providing the basis for relationship. But this does not remove us or release us from our responsibilities. His actions are so that we may then take up our part within the relationship and as the peak of creation. We have been given both admission to the covenant and a reference point to guide us towards knowing Him.

The *yods*, the *alephs* and the missing *vavs* threaded through the first four words help to refine and explain the hidden message of the opening words. The same themes and pointers emerge from examining these threads as from looking at individual words and from looking at the opening phrase as a whole in steps one to eight. We can now assemble the entry code and hear the heartbeat of creation.

Part 3
Understanding Gained

"Uncover my eyes that I may behold wonders from your Torah" (Psalm 119:18)

The first verse in Genesis poses a severe dilemma. When unpacked, these same few words provide a profound resolution and history. Details, nuances or emphases can be debated, but the form of the entry code is unmistakable; the same rhythm recurs throughout and is repeated when different approaches are taken. Through ten steps we have examined twenty-six components that cohere together in a design that meets the tough tests proposed initially.

Part Three sets out the entry code to the Hebrew Bible and shows that the message it contains is foundational. Its design precedes all and is prophetic to all of creation. The interweaving of physical and spiritual aspects gives us an inkling of how the Creator has embedded this architecture throughout creation and the call of its message within us.

The design is hidden, as the giving of the *Torah* on Mount Sinai to Moses was hidden. This hiding is for our sake. The story is incomplete. Its message confronts us with a threefold call: to knowledge, to action, and to vision. Full completion awaits our response to the question that lies at its heart.

§ § §

The Entry Code

G enesis either begins in stumbling fashion or its author provokes us to explore more deeply. It fails to begin (as one might hope) with the first letter of the Hebrew alphabet, its first word uses odd and unclear grammar, its second word partially repeats the first, and the third word is plural whilst its verb is singular. But, if we accept the author's challenge, there is no disappointment and every hope is met. If we diligently seek Him, then He can be found.

Hiding in plain view in the most visible place in the Bible, the hand of the Creator is to be found at work in His creation. Set aside the assumption that God does not reveal Himself and we discover that He does reveal Himself in the first four words. He does so with urgency and in ways that can be understood, tested and applied.

The first verse provides a path that leads to the "Here I am" of God and to the heartbeat of creation. We can hear more than the barest breath of God. He speaks so that we may know that it is He who speaks and understand and act upon what we hear.

Like archaeologists, our explorations have uncovered complexity, puzzles and seeming contradictions. We have proceeded carefully and thoroughly. The pieces we have uncovered through this process assemble together in a clear and orderly structure. Complexity, puzzles and contradictions are resolved. Though we have excavated only the foundation, its message tells us the plan and purpose of the whole. The foundation of a building is usually hidden but vital to ensuring that it remains firm, straight and true to design. So it is here. This is not some dusty artefact but a basis for our understanding and an invitation to engage.

Examining the text through a Hebraic perspective and observing strict rules has led us through twenty-six components. These provide thirty-nine separate pieces that assemble together – like pieces in a jigsaw puzzle – to provide a coherent structure. A clear picture can be seen when the pieces are combined in one particular way. The key fits the lock and the whole is a unity.

There has been some repetition in our discussion because the same or closely related points re-occur, because there are numerous inter-connections, and because the whole is tightly tied together. We are hearing the strong rhythm of the heartbeat that runs throughout creation.

A compelling composition emerges that joins all the pieces to one another so that they lock together precisely. As with a jigsaw puzzle, we can then reflexively use its architecture to test our work and see if the individual pieces have been joined correctly. Details, nuances or emphases can be debated but the form of the entry code is unmistakable. That design is embedded in the Hebrew Bible. By its nature, it is hidden, as the giving of the *Torah* on Mount Sinai to Moses was hidden from the people.

The entry code in summary

Deeply engraved in the first four words in the Bible is an inescapable design. It consists of the following elements:

A. *Division:* There is a great divide between Creator and creation. God makes Himself knowable to us through His actions in creation. Humanity is the peak of God's creation, potentially the bringer of harmony to creation.

B. *Covenant:* The great divide is overcome through covenant which makes relationship. Without this, we lack foundation for relationship with the Creator. God acts in creative power with and through those who are in covenant relationship with Him.

C.   *Messiah:* God has chosen a Messiah figure – a son – as head of His house, and cornerstone of His temple. He is the first fruits and the fulfilment of Eve's Messianic hope who links us to the Creator. He is associated both with purity and with corruption; he becomes destitute and is broken in judgement.

D.   *Sacrifice:* To be established and sustained, covenant requires blood sacrifice to stand in place of the parties to the covenant. The first fruits of creation or humanity face being cut down to provide this. However, the Lord provides on our behalf the sacrifice necessary to establish and sustain the covenant.

E.   *Exchange:* There is a Divine exchange of God's loving kindness for our failure. He shares with us the Messiah who takes upon himself the consequence of our oath breaking by providing the covenant sacrifice. God endures this loss in order to provide relationship with His creation and ensure the hope of Israel. This is no conjuring trick but the active 'I' of God crying out in woe.

F.   *Divine titles:* The first high titles given in the Bible are:

   -   *Eloha:* the Lord who takes on (our) consequences of breaking the covenant oath

   -   *Elohim:* the Lord whose suffering is concealed; He who cries out from amid the sacrifice;

   -   the son I appoint to creation (or creating), *Elohim*, the first and the last;

   -   son, son of man, son of God, the first and the last.

   As son of man, the Messiah represents us and takes on our poverty, corruption and shame. As son of God, Messiah represents God. He cries out amid the sacrifice.

G.   *His Image:* The Messiah makes real the hand of God and provides God's image to us as the basis for our participation in God's plan for creation. But there is danger of our confusing what is His with what is ours and undermining the relationship.

H.   *A sign to us:* The covenant sacrifice is the sign and seal of the New Covenant, of God-with-us. This sign of the Messiah is everlasting from first to last. God invites our participation – our 'together with' – in His plan, on the basis that He has provided.

I. *History:* Messiah is at the heart of God's plan for creation. As yet, completion is partial. Messiah is not yet fully revealed and there is hidden-ness and uncertainty. We may fail to see the active 'I' of God and instead see our own corruption and shame.

J. *Completion:* The Messiah is not consumed in the sacrifice. He will be fully revealed as the appointed head and judge of all creation at the time of the full completion. This awaits our response to the sacrifice. Then we will weep together over the price paid.

The entry code is the key to the heart of the Creator and to creation's foundation and plan. This is the message of the opening words. It is enough; it tells us what we most need to know. Each element interlocks with the others and alerts us as to what to look out for in reading the *Tanach*. Together, the elements address the core issues raised in the book of Genesis, unlock its title, provide an eternal sign, reveal hidden names and descriptions of God, and place His image within our reach.

This is no mere assertion. The entry code has been assembled through ten steps, which have found twenty–six components within the opening words, yielding forty separate points. Each element of the entry code is witnessed to by several components found within the opening words. Each of those words is a witness, repeating and confirming key elements of the message. The third word parallels the first word and the fourth word similarly parallels the second. The four different approaches used for this enquiry provide a further fourfold witness to the entry code. The different components direct our investigation of the *Tanach*, which itself gives witness to the entry code through the three levels of discussion we have pursued. In short, it all adds up.

Implications

Here is God's first principle. In a nutshell, the entry code declares that:

> The heartbeat of creation is the Creator's loving kindness
> expressed through sacrifice to make relationship.

The Creator is engaged with creation throughout history in mercy. He awaits our response in order to complete that history.

"Is not my word like fire?" declares the Lord and we have found that the fiery Torah can indeed burn. The house of creation is burning and the tree within has been set on fire by the action of God. Yet, the glory of the Lord that fills the heavens and the earth resides there. Even before the heavens or the earth are mentioned, His glory is set out in hidden form.

Beyond the austere statement of cosmology that begins the Bible we found an inherent dichotomy in the act of creation between the Creator and creation. The resolution is unfolded in that same statement. It lies in the bonds between creation and Creator established by the Creator through sacrifice, His loving kindness in action. This simple, elegant solution is stated in the beginning as the necessary foundation for creation.

The Creator proclaims "let there be" and sets in train the events of creation. The message of verse one precedes and founds those proclamations. It declares a particular kind of relationship, based on a specific dynamic that is not yet complete.

The code shows us a Creator purposefully engaged with His creation. The intent underlying His creation of the world is that He should have close relationship with, dwell with, those who have relationship with Him.[132] What is mentioned first in the Bible is the focus of His creation and the supreme demonstration of who He is. That message is inherent throughout that creation as His mercy and loving kindness is expressed.

Before Eve called, He answered. The flight of God's arrow from first creation to second is captured in the entry code. The working out of His plan rests with us. Step ten showed us how.

All this meets two more of our tests – relevance and elegance – and answers some questions:

Q: In whom can we trust?
A: In the Lord God, our Creator.

Q: How do we know this?
A: Through His loving kindness towards us, demonstrated by His word and by His covenant sacrifice.

Q: How can He trust us, who are so unworthy of trust?
A: Through His covenant sacrifice on our behalf.

---

[132] *Midrash Tanchuma, Naso* 7. Exodus 29:45 and Numbers 5:3 and 35:34 speak of the Lord dwelling with Israel. Exodus 25:8 says the construction of the tabernacle is so that He may dwell with or in them (rather than "in it"). *Midrash Tanchuma, Naso* 16 understands this to imply that He dwells in the heart of each person with whom He has covenant relationship.

Q: What then holds creation together and is the basis of close relationship between the Creator and humanity?

A: That sacrifice and the party who makes it: the heartbeat of both the Creator and of creation.

Q: How can we respond?

A: By accepting and responding to this sacrifice to fulfill our role.

Q: Why is this not made plain?

A: Because we are in the time of the partial completion, the now and the not yet. All will be fully revealed and resolved at the time of the full completion. This waits upon us and upon the time when we will weep together with the Lord.

As we have examined the first verse in the Bible, we have also been examining the first occurrence of various words, letters and concepts there. As the Vilna Gaon puts it, we have been looking at their spiritual home. Rav Tzadok HaKohen[133] states that in order to discover the profundity of an idea, we must look to the first time it appears in the *Torah*. The foundation of any concept is uncovered by analyzing it at its root, and that root is its first appearance in the *Torah*. We have seen the foundations.

The fulfilment of creation lies first with the Messiah, and then, on that basis, with us. That is the purpose of humanity being in His image. His plan, revealed in the beginning, is forward looking. Our connection with God cannot be based solely on our own righteousness. The Messiah's fulfilment of covenant opens up and maintains relationship with the Creator on our behalf. Then it is for us to make that relationship two sided and to realise it outward to the rest of creation. To deny those bonds is to deny the covenant. The covenant is established and sustained through Messiah to make us family.

There are three streams in the entry code. First, a stream that describes the core problem of creation and the Creator's provision to deal with it. Second, a stream that shows us how we are to understand and act on the first stream, each in our individual circumstances. Third, a prophetic stream that gives us the history and plan for creation so that we can collectively engage with it. To knowledge, we are to add understanding and action, and to these we are to add a collective, prophetic vision to fulfill the Creator's plan. Thus:

---

[133] Tzadok Hakohen lived 1720–1797 in Lubin, Poland.

Knowledge:

> A: Division
>
> B: Covenant
>
> C: Messiah

Understanding and action:

> D: Sacrifice
>
> E: Exchange
>
> F: Divine titles
>
> G: His image
>
> H: A sign to us

Prophetic:

> H: A sign to us (again)
>
> I: History
>
> J: Completion.

The threefold calling – to knowledge, to understanding and action, and collectively to the prophetic – is to fulfil our side of the relationship. We achieve harmony as we pick up the rhythm and make it ours.

The linchpin

Above we set out some questions and answers that flow from the entry code. In turn, it leads us to the core question:

Q: Who or what is the covenant sacrifice that provides the linchpin?

The entry code focuses on relationship provided through a covenant sacrifice, so this identity matters. From the immensity of cosmic creation, and through the complexities of the twenty-six components of the entry code, Genesis 1:1 finally directs us here. In step ten, we talked of "recovering the question": we are made in His image, so where can we look beyond ourselves to anchor this image? This led us to the Messiah, the hand of God extended towards us. As the Talmud says: "The world was created only for the sake of Messiah."[134]

---

[134] *Talmud, Sanhedrin* 98b.

This is the path we have followed:

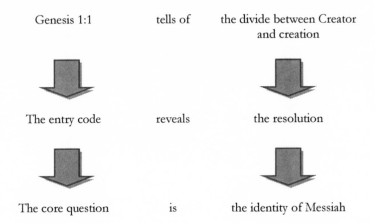

Genesis 1:1	tells of	the divide between Creator and creation
The entry code	reveals	the resolution
The core question	is	the identity of Messiah

It remains to provide the answer.

The Messiah embraces all the covenants and is the apogee of our relationship with God. He is the figure woven into the text of the first verse of Genesis and throughout the *Tanach*. We need to locate this son and Messiah who is both His and ours, the exchange point between Creator and creation, the provider of moral order, both judge and victim of judgement, and the centre point of God's first communication with us. If we can do so, we have a reference point and basis. We can begin to see the image of God and know His heart.

Is this Israel? Israel is His, God's chosen people by virtue of covenant, and consequently foremost among the nations for she serves to represent humanity before God. Israel is engraved on the palms of God's hands and He will not forget her (Isaiah 49:15–16). Israel is to be recognised by her compassion, modesty and acts of loving kindness.[135] Israel is referred to as His son, firstborn and first fruits. The covenants after Noah are with Israel and the Lord weeps over her failures. Israel has suffered much, including the Holocaust (in Hebrew *shoah*, which means 'burnt offering'). The Messiah comes from Israel.

However, Israel is part of the problem – the what-went-wrong with creation – and lacks the purity for covenant offering to the Lord. Israel is to make the Lord's name holy in the world but the Lord repeatedly has had to intervene with Israel for His name's sake (for example in Ezekiel 36). Israel fails the test of the Lord's plumb-line

---

[135] *Talmud Yebamot* 79a

(Amos 7:8) and provides us with no steadfast reference point. In terms of family, Israel is repeatedly portrayed as adulterous (for example in Judges 2:17, Psalm 106:39, and Jeremiah 2:20). The patriarchs were favoured and chosen by the Lord but also failed: the lying of Abraham and Isaac, the cunning of Jacob, the impatience of Moses. "If Thou, Lord, should mark iniquities, O Lord, who could stand?" (Psalm 130:3) Our moral order falls short.

The entry code does not lead us to Israel, or any portion of humanity as Messiah. Humanity is the pinnacle of creation but that does not mean we can fulfil the role of being His head. We are created, not Creator; we are not the singular 'I' of God; we are not the first and the last; we do not precede or embrace all of creation; we have not been sacrificed; we do not possess complete righteousness and cannot be said to be holy as the Lord is holy. To offer ourselves as covenant sacrifice is both inappropriate and forbidden.

The *vavs*, symbolising the role of man, are absent from the first four words. Their pattern of absence tells us that we are missing from the action described there, but its completion awaits our response.

The root meaning of the word for sin *(chattah)* is to 'miss' or to 'fall short of a mark'. No matter how vaunted one's view of Israel or of humanity, we all fall utterly short of the requirements and characteristics of the sacrificial figure found in Genesis 1:1. Neither our righteousness nor our suffering is sufficient for this purpose.

Discussion of human suffering is beyond the scope of this study. We can only note that it cannot by itself provide the covenant offering, no matter how great the suffering is, for it does not have the necessary characteristics. No portion of humanity, can bridge the gulf between Creator and creation on its own. That is why we are told to cry out "Create *(barah)* in me a clean heart" (Psalm 51:10).

Judaic thought understands Messiah as the righteous one who offers hope for humanity; he is the "righteous branch" of Jeremiah 23:5 and 33:15 who will save Israel and who will even be called "the Lord our righteousness." (Jeremiah 23:6).[136] Righteousness is the characteristic of Messiah; lack of righteousness belongs to us.

---

[136] This understanding of Messiah is set out in: *Talmud, Baba Bathra* 75b, *Berachot* 55b, *Sukkah* 52a, and *Sanhedrin* 98b and 99a, and in various *midrashim*. Aside from the passages in Jeremiah, other relevant Bible passages are Zechariah 9:9, Isaiah 42:6 and (more debatably) Isaiah 53:1 and, in the Apocrypha, 1 Enoch 37ff. See also footnote 131. In the view of some Hebraic writers, a few *tzaddikim* – 'righteous ones' – share the burden or prepare the way for Messiah. *Talmud Moed Katan* 28a says that "the death of the righteous brings atonement".

The kingdom of heaven is longed for but is not yet.[137]

> God has looked down from heaven upon the sons of
> men, to see if there is anyone who understands, who
> seeks after God. Every one of them has turned aside;
> together they have become corrupt; there is no one who
> does good, not even one.   Psalm 53:2–3

The hope of a personal Messiah remains a strong theme in Judaism.[138]
To continue with Psalm 53: "Oh, that out of Zion would come Israel's
salvation" (verse 7). Many in Zion continue to await that salvation.

Genesis 1:1 tells us of the Messiah who provides our
righteousness before God and who provides to us the image of God.
This is the *sheth* figure – the son of God, son of man – mediating
between God and man. He and no other provides our righteousness
before God. Here the kingdom of heaven is brought near to us. Here
is the active 'I' of God with us.

> I, even I, am the one who wipes out your transgressions,
> for My own sake; and I will not remember your sins.
> Isaiah 43:25

This is the Lord whose suffering is concealed: *el-hy-m*. Even as *Elohim* is
introduced as the third word of the Bible, the construction of the word
itself speaks of the nature of this sacrifice and suffering. This offers us
far more than the barest breath of the knowledge of God.

The blood of sacrifice is placed at the entry to the Bible, as the
blood of a sacrificed lamb was smeared at the entry to each family
home at the Passover before Israel's flight from Egypt. As at that first
Passover, there is a promise of life instead of death and of freedom
through the blood that makes atonement (Leviticus 17:11).

God's loving kindness, expressed through His fulfilment of
covenant, gives us the basis and form for our own actions. We can join
with Him through covenant and reflect that outward to others. The

---

[137] See also Psalm 14:3, Psalm 53:2, Isaiah 41:28, and Ecclesiastes 7:20.

[138] Maimonides takes a narrow view of the role of Messiah but nonetheless states
"Whoever does not believe in him, or does not await his coming, denies not only the
prophets, but also the Torah and Moses" *Mishneh Torah, Sefer Shoftim,* 11.1. A
statement for the Hasidim (a major movement within contemporary Judaism) is
"The Moshiach is a person. The Hasidim never accept the notion of a Messianic age
apart from a personal Moshiach", Rabinowicz, Tzvi (Ed.) (1996) *Encyclopaedia of
Hasidim,* Aronson, p312.

invitation is both to join with and to reflect outward. It is an invitation to fulfil our purpose in creation and it is founded on the Messiah.

The entry code tells us that the son of man, son of God, the head of the house, is the costly cornerstone, the eternal foundation, the first and the last, God's lament and destitution. He enters into creation and takes on our humanity to become the first fruits of many, dedicated and sacrificed on behalf of the many. We are the many; he is the one.

The entry code also tells us that the Messiah figure must die in sacrifice. For him to become the complete completion, to be both first and last, he must then return to life.[139] The Messiah must come, the Messiah must die a sacrificial death, and then the Messiah must return to life. This is hidden from many. His sacrifice is not yet fully revealed until that final completion. For the present, man can corrupt how this appears to us. All this too is contained in the message of the entry code. God hides His actions. In consequence we are given choices in how to fulfill our side of the relationship: we can ignore it altogether and follow our own path or we can seek the Divine path.

A Stumbling Point

The signals and implications of the entry code hidden at the beginning of the *Tanach* are now clear. But that to which they lead is a stumbling point. The message of the entry code is a direct challenge. Provocation lies in the beginning. Deuteronomy 6:7 tells us to sharpen or pierce *(shanan)* the word of God to our sons. The word is not intended to be soothing. We are to be pierced by its truth.

This enquiry has drawn from the Hebrew Bible and Hebraic insights. Looking to these sources and using Hebraic approaches to Scripture yields the entry code that unlocks the meta-narrative of the *Tanach*. We have not drawn from the Messianic writings that are collectively known as the 'New Testament', nor used typical Christian approaches to exegesis. Yet, what we have found could suggest the

---

[139] The death and resurrection of a Messiah figure are suggested in the *Talmud, Sukkah* 52a: "But when he will see that the Messiah, the son of Joseph, is slain, he will say to Him 'Lord of the Universe, I ask Thee only the gift of life'. 'As to life, He would answer him, 'Your father David has already prophesied this concerning you', as it is said, 'He asked life of thee, thou gavest it him." The reference is to Psalm 21:4/5. Death and resurrection of Messiah could be implied by the hiding and reappearance of Messiah in some Judaic literature: see footnote 119.

crucifixion and resurrection of Christ and the sign of the cross.[140] Could the cross of Jesus Christ – *Yeshua ha Messiach*, literally 'Saviour, the Messiah' – be the sign of God with us in the New Covenant?

The whole thrust of the message in the entry code is to a figure and sign and action that appear to correspond with that figure and sign and action. What are we to make of this? Three areas need to be examined: the nature of the correspondence; the outworking in practice; and the implications for the future. These broadly correspond to the threefold division of the entry code into knowledge, understanding and action, and the prophetic.

The nature of the connection and the knowledge provided through the entry code:

'New Testament' means 'New Covenant' (in Greek *diatheke* is used to mean both 'covenant' and 'testament'). The Messianic writings that are called the 'New Testament' are predominantly Jewish in origin and outlook, based on Hebraic streams of interpretation of Scripture current in the 1st Century CE, and explicate their authors' understanding of the realization of the New Covenant. These writings have a 'meta-narrative': a big, overarching story. The essentials of that story coincide with the entry code outlined here.

Subsequent Christian approaches to the Hebrew Bible (the so called 'Old Testament') have often imposed a later view of the meta-narrative of the New Testament that has drawn it far away from its Hebraic roots, and then applied that later view to interpreting pieces of the Hebrew Scriptures. This study has proceeded in exactly the opposite direction, beginning at the beginning and examining the first verse of the Hebrew Bible in the context of the *Tanach* and Judaic perspectives. It is an Hebraic study of the Hebrew Bible using Hebrew sources under strict rules, with multiple witnesses and subject to a battery of tests. If we set aside its core findings, then we set aside that Hebraic approach and ignore the first occurrence and 'spiritual home' of key words and concepts in the *Tanach*.

Yet, all of the elements A to J of the entry code, indeed all the points previously discussed, harmonise with the meta-narrative of the Messianic writings, provided that those writings are understood from a Hebraic perspective and as being based on the *Tanach*. The components found within the opening words and the elements of the entry code as a whole insistently lead us to the same message

---

[140] In the Proto-Sinaitic script, the letter for the Hebrew *tav* – the second letter of the *aleph-tav* – was formed as a +

concerning Messiah as the Messianic writings known as the New Testament. Both speak of the Messiah and *Elohim* and the New Covenant in parallel ways.

The strength and exactness of this parallel are striking, including the oneness of the Creator (discussed at step six) and the ongoing centrality of Israel to His plan for creation. The correspondence between the two is hard to ignore, both in terms of the overall picture and in terms of detail, such as use of the terms 'son of man' and 'son of God' identified in component (w). The central act for both accounts is the sacrifice of a blameless Messianic figure on a tree for our sake. In component (p), we even found that the name of God, *Eloha* (singular), that lies within *Elohim* (plural), is tied to His taking on the curse from breaking a covenant oath in the context of a tree.

The simplest solution to the similarity of the two accounts is that they are, in fact, the same: both concern the same person, sign and action. This would also fulfil one more of our ten tests: that the message of the entry code should be connected to actual events. The parallel will be considered further in the Conclusions where some details and examples from the Messianic writings will be looked at. Alternative explanations are discussed in Appendix C. Whether the discovery is welcome or expected is not the issue. If this is the word of God in the beginning, the consequences must be addressed: by looking at the *Tanach* and the Messianic writings together from a shared perspective, we can comprehend what the Lord is saying to us. In short, it can all make sense.

The outworking:

For many the sign of the New Testament or New Covenant has not been good news. At times it has been a symbol of attack upon His chosen people, demonstrating the hostility and inhumanity of man rather than the love of God. The cross has been made repugnant through acts carried out under that sign by some who claim to represent Christ.

Sadly, this should not surprise us. The failings of human beings should not be confused with what they claim to represent. Our morality falls short of His; accordingly our failures are not His. Such falling short is demonstrated in the history of Christianity. Similarly, in the *Tanach*, the Jewish people, as God's chosen people, at times bring the name of God into disrepute, forcing Him to act to discipline them "for My name's sake". Israel does not cease to be His people, nor does He cease to be Israel's God. Rather, such weakness illustrates our need for God's mercy. God remains true, even if we do not. (Nor should we overlook the many positives in the history of Christianity or of Israel. Otherwise, we are engaged in mere polemics.)

God has taken on Himself the consequences of our failure to fulfil covenant. The entry code tells us what is His, what is shared and what are our responsibilities. In step ten, we suggested that religious error stems from taking what is His for our own possession. If we lose understanding of what is His, what is ours and what is shared, then we become confused and can fall into corruption. We can no longer represent him and He can no longer operate through us. Hence, the Lord will tear down the house of the proud (Proverbs 15:25).

If we seize what is His, then we will be crushed or crush others by precisely those responsibilities that He has relieved us from because we cannot bear them. Those who take His tree or His fire or His oath and imagine that they own or control it will go astray. Hence, when the cross is treated as a symbol of our own power or knowledge, it can no longer point to the covenant sacrifice that He chose to make on our behalf. Its significance is lost. Similarly where the cross is taken to illustrate the failure of some particular group – for example, to condemn 'the Jews' – we can no longer find there His universal answer to our universal need. Instead of leading to Him, our folly turns the cross into something that leads us away.

The dualities of the entry code warn of such dangers. Components (k) and (p) show us that the tree is a place of danger and failure as well as of hope and rebirth. We can choose to see the Divine or to see human corruption in the sacrifice made by Messiah for us. We can choose to see only sinful Cain, only the destitution and shame. Yet, the confusion and corruption are ours, not God's, and are why a gift of homage is needed. Only when we recognise His hand extend towards us can relationship with God flow. The tragedy of history is the loss of that relationship.

That much of Israel should miss or misunderstand the Messiah and the fulfilment of covenant fits both with the warnings, uncertainties and dualities presented by the entry code and with the history of Israel's struggles at they are recorded in the *Tanach*. Israel fell to worshipping the golden calf whilst Moses received the Law on Mount Sinai; King David faced a major revolt although he had received an enduring covenant; Jeremiah, the prophet of the New Covenant, was imprisoned and thrown down a cistern by the leadership of his day; and so on. These events are both history and a prophetic warning.

Christianity has also stumbled in understanding and representing His image. Again, we all fall short.

From the beginning, the entry code prophesies these failures. As we discussed in step nine, Israel is liable to miss the active I of God at work in creation and consequently not understand the sign, the lament, the entry to the temple, the brokenness, the tree or the destitution of the head of the house. Because of this, there is no completion as yet. This does not mean the permanent rejection of Israel anymore than her previous failures did. The New Covenant is with Israel (Jeremiah 32:31) and therefore its completion awaits Israel.

The covenant is fresh to each generation. The path has been prepared and signposts mark the way for each of us and for each generation. The Ark of the Covenant and the temple are long lost but we can still find He who is the covenant for all of creation, He who is God with us, He who is the first and the last. As we find – or rediscover – Him, we gain our basis for understanding and for action, whatever the world or our culture may say and whatever the mistaken actions of some who lay claim to represent Him.

This is the relevance of the entry code <u>now</u>, both to those who are of Israel and those who are not. Rather than trying to assume His responsibilities, it is time to assume our own. There is a time to fathom what God has done for us and to accept the sign of the *aleph-tav*. "For this commandment which I give you today is not too difficult for you, nor is it out of reach." (Deuteronomy 30:11)

Implications for the future:

We are in the time of incompleteness; there is uncertainty. We should not be taken aback for Ecclesiastes 3:11 says:

> He has made everything beautiful in its own time. He has set eternity (or enigma) in the hearts of men, yet they cannot fathom what God has done from the beginning to the end.

With our hearts we search for that which is hidden. The *aleph-tav* – the sign of the beginning to the end, the sign of the New Covenant – is hard to fathom. The same verse provides hope for it promises that everything is beautiful in its own time. Our lack of understanding is not inescapable. Elsewhere, the *Tanach* looks forward to the beauty of Messiah and the beauty of saved Israel (Zechariah 9:16/17).

To bring completion and beauty to His plan rests with us, and in particular with Israel. Israel is told to be holy and is set apart from the nations (Leviticus 20:26; Exodus 19:5–6). Just as the Lord weeps over Israel, Jeremiah prophesies that Israel and Judah:

> ... will go along weeping as they go, and it will be the Lord their God they seek ... they will come that they may join themselves to the Lord in an everlasting covenant that will not be forgotten. My people have become lost sheep. Their shepherds have led them astray.   Jeremiah 50:4–6

The people of Israel have mostly still to recognise that sign of the first and the last, to accept that lament and destitution which provides for joining with God, and thus to join that everlasting covenant. The active 'I' of God awaits that rejoining with Israel in everlasting covenant, the New Covenant, so that His creative power can again be poured out on Israel. Then the Lord says:

> I will pour out on the house of David and on the inhabitants of Jerusalem, the Spirit of grace and of supplication, so that they will look on me whom they have pierced, and they will mourn for him, as one mourns for an only son, and they will weep bitterly over him, like the bitter weeping over a first-born.
> Zechariah 12:10[141]

It has been said that "*Torah* remains the key to all the secrets and resources of creation."[142] By so treating the first four words of *Torah*, we have discovered an entire theology and an everlasting bond. This is a relationship with the Creator that will not be forgotten and to which Israel is called: the history and nub of creation, both the name of God and the familiar statement "In the beginning God created..."

---

[141] Translations of this passage vary. *Talmud, Sukkah* 52a views this passage as speaking of the Messiah, as do Rashi, Ibn Ezra and Moses Alshech. Of these, all but Alshech see the piercing as done by the gentiles.

[142] R Scherman, Nosson (1986) "Overview", in *Bereishis: Genesis. A New Translation with a Commentary Anthologized from Talmudic, Midrashic and Rabbinic Sources, Vol 1a, ArtScroll Tanach,* Mesorah, N.Y. p xxxii.

Conclusions

W hat is the meaning for us of what we have found? We have discovered the message of the entry code. As part of the journey, our enquiry into the first four words has:

- revealed an eternal sign

- placed within reach the image – His image – in which we are created

- decoded the first name of God in the Bible

- identified the first adjective describing the nature of God

- unpacked the title of the first book in the *Torah*

- provided several hidden names of God

- helped grasp mysterious Biblical texts, such as the eternal name and sign of God introduced to Moses at the burning bush.

These are not isolated findings or peculiar interpretations. By combining all our findings, the entry code is revealed. Together they yield a rich and coherent composition that resolves the insistent themes and questions that recur at different levels and throughout the different approaches adopted.

But, if this is so useful to our understanding of the Hebrew Bible, why is the message hidden; why the need for investigation?

In times past, some have forbidden the divulgence of mysteries from within the opening passages of Genesis.[143] But there comes a time to speak, a time to unveil our eyes, for "He has made everything beautiful in its own time". When the rulers howl and there is continual blasphemy, in that day we are to look for Him and to know His Name (Isaiah 52:5–6). These are the birth pangs of Messiah.

If the key was not given in times past, it has been given to us.

> You have heard; look at all this and you, will you not
> declare it! I proclaim to you new things from this time,
> even hidden things which you have not known.
> Isaiah 48:6

These matters are not secret; the hiding is not permanent. Isaiah 48:16 says "From the first *(reish-aleph-shin)*, I have not spoken in secret." Genesis 1:1 is first and it contains *reish-aleph-shin* within its very first word. Isaiah tells us that this opening message in the Bible is not spoken in secret; it is not of those secret things that belong to God alone (Deuteronomy 29:29). Instead, it is to be declared. There is no alternative.

The uncertainty and concealment are for our sake:

> the secret of the Lord is for those who fear Him, and
> He will make them know His covenant.
> Psalm 25:14

To know His covenant is not straightforward; knowledge is not 'on demand'. The Lord longs that Israel:

> …may see and observe and consider and gain insight as
> well, that the hand *(yod)* of the Lord has done this, and
> the Holy One of Israel has created *(barah)* it.
> Isaiah 41:20

The progression of verbs – to see, then observe, then consider, and then gain insight – suggests the struggle and effort necessary if we are to grasp the *yod* (the hand) of the Lord. We have to progress from knowledge to understanding to insight into the prophetic.

---

[143] See footnote 4.

From the beginning, the Bible allows dualities rather than certainty. From the beginning, the presence of God is veiled. There is a concealed part of God's rule. The *aleph* that is the active 'I' of the Creator in creation is no more than a breath.

The text confronts us. It prompts us either to seek His hand or to rely on our own knowledge and power; either to desire His provision for us or to choose to remain where we are. The full completion awaits our decision and our determined pursuit of Him. Yet, His hand is always extended toward us in creative power, even from the beginning. That is the meaning for us of what we have found

Finding the entry code has taken diligence and adherence to strict rules. We have taken the letters and words of Genesis 1:1 in the order they come, including words folded within words. We have only considered words and meanings of words that occur in the *Tanach*. We have interpreted Genesis 1:1 and related passages from the Hebrew Bible in terms of each other and through Hebraic understanding. Any individual component taken alone may appear insignificant or dubious or merely puzzling. However, each of the components reinforces and substantiates the others.

Together they reveal what lies within Genesis 1:1 and compose a rich and detailed architecture. The entry code passes all the tests outlined at the start of our enquiry: inclusiveness, precision, coherence, robustness, appropriateness, power, relevance, elegance, connection and uniqueness. The last test is a challenge. The entry code uniquely configures the components of the first four words and connects them to a unique set of real events. Can the reader find a viable alternative way to assemble those components that meets all the tests?

The heartbeat of creation

The entry code to the Bible declares that the heartbeat of creation is the Creator's loving kindness expressed through sacrifice to make relationship. All that follows can be read – is to be searched and understood – in this light. Here is where God is to be found.

Einstein is said to have asked if God had a choice in creating the universe. The entry code shows that there was a critical choice: a moral choice not a physical one. The basis of creation is the moral order set by the Creator's decision. This comes first. The creation of the physical heavens and the physical earth embodies that Divine order: "The heavens declare the glory of God." (Psalm 19:1). Consequently, a moral order and moral choice face us.

The first phrase in the Bible interweaves the physical and the spiritual. This interweaving revealed by the entry code gives us an inkling of how the moral order of salvation is embedded in all of creation and is the target of time's arrow. That design precedes all and is prophetic to all of creation. It provides the rhythm for creation and the 'programme code' for the universe. "Even the world in all its entirety is not equivalent to a single word of *Torah*."[144]

Creation's heartbeat unites the material universe and our internal moral world in the Creator's purpose. We are a microcosm of the macro. The Creator's heartbeat is creation's heartbeat, and ours too, from the first. Yet it is incomplete. Completion awaits our response to the relationship God offers us. We are responsible for that decision.

The message reveals the particulars of the glory of God. It shows the way in which each of us can fully realize our humanity and Israel can be all that she has been called to be. There is a threefold call: to knowledge, to action, and collectively to the prophetic. Behind the vast cosmological statement at the opening of Genesis, the code provides a gateway to the whole book and to comprehending the Creator's plan.

A severe dilemma is posed by the first verse in the Bible. When unpacked, these same few words provide a profound resolution. The overwhelming themes are the divide between Creator and creation and how the Creator bridges this gulf and maintains relationship with His creation through covenant sacrifice. To understand these two themes ands their outworking in history is to understand God's heartbeat for His creation and thus creation's heartbeat for Him. That is why the entry code is contained within the Bible's description of the first creative act. The heartbeat is the Messiah who provides the bridge. To discover that heartbeat is to discover who we are.

The covenant sacrifice comes not from creation but from God. If we come upon corruption and destitution and murder, they come from us, not from God. The Messiah takes all that on himself. This taking on is the purpose and cost of the sacrifice. God's loss is great. Our own failures, mistakes, and terrors, however great, are taken out of the way – swallowed up – if we will permit that.

> "Come now and let us reason together" says the Lord.
> "Though your sins are as red as scarlet, they will be as
> white as snow."   Isaiah 1:18

Through this, kinship with Him becomes possible.

---

[144] *Jerusalem Talmud, Peah,* 1:4.

There is yet time. The entry code shows us that we live in the era of the partial completion. God calls to us, as He has always called to Israel and to the nations. He will make known His covenant. The entry to the temple of God's presence beckons us to be together with Him for the Lord is with us.

All of the pain and all of the failure of human history and of our individual lives find resolution in the passage back to God through the bridge that He has provided in Messiah. The bridge is not for us to build but for us to cross. Our highest fulfilment is to favourably reflect and realize what is shown to us in and through the son who fulfils the covenant. This is the core of His message to us, the illustration and outworking of His moral order for all of creation. This is the basis on which life is worth living and the context for our good deeds.

We have discovered God's goal in history. From all the complexity and detail that this enquiry has uncovered, finally it becomes simple. From the vast span of God's actions, the focus narrows down to a single figure and a single series of actions. All creation and all of time revolve around this. That is what God tells us in the beginning. The centre is the moment in time of the actual covenant sacrifice of the Messiah, son of man, son of God.

The message made public

The message is both concealed and has been made very public in the most public sacrifice of all time. This enquiry has not needed or relied on the Messianic writings that are called the New Testament. Yet, what has been found through Hebraic techniques and perspective is what those writings speak of when they are understood from such a perspective. What we find is the secret of the Lord: "the mystery which has been hidden from the ages and the generations, but has now been manifested" (Colossians 1:26). The entire code, with its twenty-six component parts, points inevitably and unequivocally to the Messiah as *Yeshua ha Mashiach* ('Saviour, the Messiah' which has become 'Jesus Christ' in English). Only He can satisfy its twin themes and fulfil the different components revealed in our enquiry.

The Ark of the Covenant once stood in the Holy of Holies at the centre of the temple in Jerusalem. It was the focus for the presence of God and contained the Mosaic covenant, representing the close covenant bond between Israel and God. The ark has vanished but we have uncovered at the centre of the temple of all creation something better: a figure who is the presence of God with us, and who is the covenant and basis of relationship with God for all creation.

This is no theoretical construct or something locked away. The outworking is described from a Hebraic perspective by the Messianic writings of the New Testament. At times these writers seem directly to exposit Genesis 1:1; for example: the opening of John's gospel – "In the beginning was the Word and the Word was with God" – or the opening of Paul's letter to the Ephesians which speaks of the "summing up of all things in Christ, things in the heavens and things upon the earth." Paul speaks of being a "new creature" or "new creation" in Christ (2 Corinthians 5:17; Galatians 6:15), bringing us back to Genesis 1:1 and a new creation through the figure of the son.

Detail in the *Tanach* matters and we have found that even the little *yods* have much to tell us. We can see why *Yeshua ha Mashiach* said that "until heaven and earth pass away not the smallest letter *(yod)* or stroke shall pass away from the Law (the *Torah*) until all is accomplished." (Matthew 5:18)

This enquiry and the Messianic writings share a common platform in that they draw on understandings of the *Torah* from the 1stC CE and earlier (and, in our case, as reflected in later writings). Neither is about foreign gods. Pursuing in detail the links between the *Tanach* and the later Messianic writings in the New Testament is beyond our scope. We have found a meta-story embedded in the first verse of the Hebrew Bible. That meta-story connects to and is echoed by the Messianic writings of the New Testament. The findings of this enquiry point at every level to *Yeshua ha Mashiach* of the New Testament. Indeed, many of the points we have found are also unfolded there with specific reference to *Yeshua*. Here are some examples.

In terms of description and knowledge:

In its opening verse, it is stated to be the book of the *genesis* (Greek) of *Iesus Christos*, son of David, son of Abraham. (Matthew 1:1)

He is the one whom Moses in the *Torah* and the prophets wrote about. (John 1:45) He says "all things which are written about Me in the Law of Moses, and the Prophets and the Psalms must be fulfilled". (Luke 24:44)

The titles "son of man" and "son of God" are repeatedly used of him.

He is described as the firstborn of all creation. (Colossians 1:15). In the last chapter of the last book of the New Testament, He uses the title "first and last" of Himself, referring back to the *aleph-tav* in the opening phrase of Genesis. (Revelations 22:13)

In terms of 'the son I appoint to creation', He is described as God's gift to us, "for He gave His only son". (John 3:16).

His works have come into being from the foundation of the world. (Hebrews 4:3)

"His name is called the word of God" and as the word He was God and was in the beginning with God. (Revelations 19:13, John 1:1).

His name is Emmanuel, God with us. (Matthew 1:23)

He repeatedly states that "the kingdom of heaven is at hand". (Matthew 4:17)

He refers to Himself as a grain of wheat that must die and the bread of life and is described as the first fruits. (John 12:23–24, John 6:35, 6:48, 1 Corinthians 15:20, 23). He is the hope of Israel. (Acts 28:20)

He is the mediator of the New Covenant. (Hebrews 9:15) He refers to "the New Covenant in my blood". (Luke 22:20, 1 Corinthians 11:25)

In terms of understanding and action:

The Word became flesh and dwelt among us. (John 1:14)

He became poor for us. (2 Corinthians 8:9) He says He is the cornerstone rejected by the builders. (Ps 118:22; Mt 21:42)

His message must first be given to the Jews. (Matthew 15:24; Romans 1:16; 2:10)

His actions reveal the righteousness of God. (Romans 1:17; 3:21–22). Through Him, we can grasp in whose image we are created. (Colossians 1:15; Philippians 2:6-7; Hebrews 1:3). God is not unknown but has called us to repentance. (Acts17:22–31)

He identified Himself with the Father: "He who has seen me has seen the Father … I am in the Father and the Father is in Me." (John 14:11–13)

He was silent before His accusers. (Matthew 26:63, Matthew 27:12–13, Acts 8:32) But He lamented His own suffering. (Luke 22:41–44; Matthew 27:46).

He was stripped of his outer garments and crowned with thorns. On the cross, He was shamed and mocked by both gentile and Jew, yet endured the cross and despised the shame. (John 19:23–24; Matthew 27:29, 41; Hebrews 12:2)

His body was broken for us. (1 Corinthians 11:24) He became a curse for us on a tree. (Galatians 3:13)

He is to be a sacrifice on our behalf, "God ... sending His own son ... as an offering for sin". (Romans 8:3). He took on our sin: "He made Him who knew no sin to be sin on our behalf". (2 Corinthians 5:21) For this reason God exalted Him and His name above all others. (Philippians 2:9)

He is the substitute for temple sacrifices. (Hebrews 7:26–28) The temple curtain to the Holy of Holies was torn in two when He died. (Matthew 27:51)

Without His sacrifice, gentiles are strangers to the covenants and without God in the world. (Ephesians 2:12)

He entered the holy place of a more perfect tabernacle than the earthly one through His own blood and once and for all. (Hebrews 9: 11–12)

All this gives us hope and makes us adequate as servants and ministers of a new covenant (2 Corinthians 3:5-11). We are a new creature in Him; we are His ambassadors with His righteousness and carrying the word of reconciliation. (2 Corinthians 5:19-21)

In terms of the future:

Speaking of Israel: "what will their acceptance (of Messiah) be but life from the dead?" (Romans 11:15)

He will one day return in the glory of His Father, that is, as the son of God. (Matthew 25:31; Mark 8:38)

The whole of creation groans and suffers the pains of childbirth. It will be set free from corruption into the freedom of the glory of the children of God. (Romans 8:19–23)

He will judge the living and the dead. (2 Timothy 4:1) But there is no condemnation for those who are in Him. (Romans 8:1)

All things in heaven and earth will be summed up in the Messiah. (Ephesians 1:10)

No created thing can separate us from the love of God which is in *Yeshua ha Mashiach*. (Romans 8:39)

When we consider the entry code in terms of this material even the detail is telling. For example, *Eloha* (singular) is identified with taking on the curse of the covenant oath whilst *Elohim* (plural) cries out over the cost of this. This shows the nature of God involved in that sacrifice on the cross through the Son: *Eloha* takes on the curse and *Elohim* – the unity of the Godhead – suffers.

The opening of Genesis and the content of the New Testament together provide a dual testimony to the message that they each contain. A third stream of evidence is added by the real events that fulfil what was prophesied from the beginning.

The Messiah did all this for love. His action provides the model for us: "Be imitators of God, as beloved children, and live in love, as Christ loved us and gave himself up for us, an offering and a sacrifice to God." (Ephesians 5:1-2)

We are all familiar with His death on the cross, a tree. Genesis 1:1 confirms His central significance for all creation; He is our foundation and cornerstone. The horrific abuses carried out under the sign of the cross over the centuries alter none of this. Indeed, they show how much we all need Him. The *shin* can identify corruption, the Messiah can expose the murderous heart, just as the laws of the Mosaic covenant uncovered the sinfulness of Israel.

"Who has believed our message? And to whom has the arm of the Lord been revealed?" (Isaiah 53:1) We have found the Messiah, the son of God, son of man. This is the son who is placed at the centre of all the acts of creation: from creation week to God's ongoing and future creative acts, whether towards His chosen people, Israel, or toward a people yet to be created. This is the son who is at the centre of God's family and of the covenant. We have discovered in Genesis 1:1 the foundation for all these and the basis for creation's relationship with its Creator. The Messiah can be found and the bridge he provides for creation back to the Creator is available to us now. Each of us can become a new creation in Him.

What holds back the conclusion of the Divine composition and the revelation of *Elohim* throughout creation? The entry code is a call to action, a call to accept the yoke of the kingdom of heaven. The Messiah says: "Take My yoke upon you... for My yoke is easy and my

load is light." (Matthew 11:29–30)[145]   The waiting is for us to accept
and act on His covenant sacrifice; in particular for its acceptance by
those with whom the covenant was made: Israel.   As God's chosen
people, Israel is called to the knowledge of God and to spread that
knowledge.   In his Messianic writings, Paul of Tarsus says that when
Israel accepts that knowledge then "it will be life from the dead" for
the world (Romans 11:15).   The creative power of God will be released.
The fulfilment of this calling remains; the task of Israel awaits:

> then I shall be sanctified through them in the sight of
> the many nations... And I will not hide My face from
> them any longer.   Ezekiel 39:27–29

If this is the entry code, it must be tested.   The start of this enquiry
advanced two propositions in the form of questions:

- A proposition for the mind: Is this message contained within
  Genesis 1:1?   How can this be and what light does it throw on
  what follows?

- A proposition for the heart: Is this significant: does it speak to
  our deepest need and to the pain and suffering of our world?
  Does this move us beyond despair?

We need to consider what has been found and determine its truth.

The first and most urgent message of the Bible may be unfamiliar
and disturbing to our own worldview or individual narrative.   But the
question is its truth, not its convenience.   Because the message contains
that uncertainty which allows for human quest and decision and choice,
it gives each reader the space to determine matters for themselves.   As
always, it is up to us.   Here are some thoughts on the two propositions.

Proposition for the mind

We have sought to discover if and how the Creator speaks to us in the
beginning.   As we discussed in the opening chapter, there is a logical
and methodical means of doing so.   Unlike the atheist's denial of the
possibility of communication from the Creator, this is testable.

Plato remarked that "God is always doing geometry".[146]   Such a
view implies that we could understand Him through study of design in

---

[145] In context, "yoke" would have been understood to refer to the interpretation of
Torah being advanced.

[146] Plutarch, *Moralia, Quaest. Conv.*

the external world. Genesis 1:1 gives much more than the beginning of physical geometry or the origin of the 'big bang'. We have uncovered a complex, multi-level, fractal geometry: the geometry of love that encompasses creation, the heartbeat that sets the rhythm for all of creation. But how do we test that which is not measurable?

Contained within the sixteen letters of the first four words, we have found some twenty different words with over thirty different meanings, together with seven Hebrew letters that stand alone or modify the significance of the words. The strict rules we have used in this exploration limit the number of permutations that can occur without breaking those rules. We have used different approaches and discovered that they confirm each other through diverse witnesses.

What we have found joins together precisely, coherently, and robustly into a logical and profound structure that sheds light on the wider text of the Hebrew Bible and on its specific context at its beginning. It meets the criteria and tests set out at the start of our enquiry. Within the method adopted and the firm limits that we have imposed, this – and no other geometry – is what we have found. Only this key fits and opens the door.

Under tight constraints, we have examined what the opening of the Bible tells us. We have seen the complexity, depth and central import of what is revealed through the twenty-six components that we have uncovered within the tiny frame of four words. Layer upon layer of significance and hints have been explored. These interlock with the rest of the Bible and provide a map to navigate God's unfolding plan.

This message is deeply entwined with the most controversial event in history and the most influential and famous person in history. In terms of the ninth of our ten tests, the entry code is connected to actual events and issues. It is prophetic, accurate and specific.

Could anyone but the Creator arrange such a grand geometry and such an intricate message to be hidden in the first four words of His communication to us? In that statement, the very fabric of the Semitic languages is used to convey the nature of creation. It is as if these languages were constructed to speak in this way, and in such subtle and intricate rhythms. Having done that, could anyone but the Creator God who continues to be involved with His creation provide for the precise fulfilment of this message 2,000 years ago in Jerusalem,[147] and for the sign of this to be the most well known sign of all time?

---

[147] Scholars agree that the *Tanach,* the Hebrew Bible, was completed hundreds of years before the events described in the New Testament.

Whether this is convenient or fits with preconceived notions does not alter its truth. We need to consider if it true because it is for us to align ourselves with God and with His word, not the other way around.

But, there is a double difficulty. The reader faces the apparent absence of God, the concealment of His reign, the association of what is good with what is evil, and the binary choices within the code. And the reader faces the stumbling block of history that we discussed in the previous chapter: the failure in witness and outworking of some who said that they received His message.

The code is simple and clear, yet leaves us with uncertainties and choices. This lack of certainty does not suggest that there is lack of evidence or that we cannot respond. Rather, we are confronted as to how to respond. The key opens the door but it is for us to walk through. This in itself is evidence of its truth. The Creator shows how and why He leaves the summit of his creation, humanity, free to choose our own path. That path is either towards or away from Him.

We do not claim to have every minute detail of our discussion correct or, even at such length, to have carried out a complete study. But has our exploration been fundamentally mistaken or flawed? The reader is invited to consider the objections discussed in Appendix C and to take up the challenge of the last of the ten tests; to find an alternative way to bring together the components discovered that meets the strict criteria of this enquiry.

Each reader will decide for themselves the claim of this message or geometry: whether it is true or false, prophesy or nonsense, the path to intimacy with the Creator or to false worship, life changing or minor amusement. Have we found something or nothing? If nothing, then our attempt to study the opening words of the Bible has left ashes in our mouths. It is as if the author of those words wished to mislead or block deeper enquiry, even in the beginning. Is this our God? If something, then the beginning of Genesis is exactly what it claims to be: our foundation and key to our history and future. Consequently, its fulfilment 2,000 years ago is the centre of creation, of history and of our relationship with God. The love of God can be found.

The opening words contain a threefold call: to knowledge, to action and to the prophetic. The response to each, and the responsibility for each, rests with each of us. To find out more, read the book – the *Tanach* and the Messianic writings known as the New Testament – with an open mind and an open spirit:

Proposition for the heart

The second proposition asks: Is what we have found significant; does it speak to our deepest need and to the pain and suffering of the world?

This is not a matter of immediate or superficial reaction, but what speaks at the deepest level to our innermost being. We may imagine that we know what we most need from God and consequently what He should do for us. But, if this is the first and most urgent message to us, then it is what we most need to hear, what we most need to know and what we most need to act on. It tells us what we have always most needed to know from the beginning. Then, it invites our response.

It may be almost unbearable, but is this the heart of God that shows us how we can begin to be fulfilled, how He can enter into our personal history as we connect with Him? Does it encourage us to have hope? Does this understanding of God's heartbeat and word open a path that can satisfy the soul, make the simple wise, rejoice the heart, enlighten the eyes and taste sweeter than honey (Psalm 19)?

The purpose of Hebrew *aggadah* (telling) is to touch the human heart so that we can recognise He who created the world and cling to His ways.[148] Judaism's daily prayer, *Alenu*, speaks of:

> our hope, O Lord our God, that we may soon see the glory of Your power to remove abominations from the earth so that idols are utterly cut off, to perfect the world under the sovereignty of the Almighty.

In Hebrew, the phrase "to perfect the world" can be read as speaking of a hidden or concealed healing. The entry code speaks of this concealed healing and perfection. It shows us the foundation of all creation in God's loving kindness. It shows us how to turn from relying on our idols to relying on Him. God accepts the offering of His own son as the necessary breaking in judgment of a gift from creation. Can we accept the price He paid and become "conformed to the image of His Son, that He might be the firstborn among many brethren" (Romans 8:29)? Do we want to be family on such terms?

Often we can react against that which is acceptable to God: Cain slew Abel because Abel's offering was acceptable to God. Eternity is in our hearts but the heart searches for God on its own terms.

The opening words of the Bible show us both the great divide between Creator and creation and how God becomes knowable in His

---

[148] *Talmud Yoma* 75a, *Sifre Devarim* 49.

creative power. When the pinnacle of creation – humanity – fails, He makes Himself known through the Messiah: love in action. His geometry of love provides and sustains the covenant to which we can be party if we choose. We are told both to love and to fear the Lord. The entry code sets out the basis and necessity for both and demonstrates that His mercy overrules all.

The covenant both provides relationship with Father God and remakes family. As we turn to Him on that basis, there can be a release of His creative power to bring us into alignment with the Creator.

> One thing I have desired of the Lord, that shall I seek:
> that I may dwell in the house of the Lord all the days of
> my life, to behold the beauty of the Lord and to
> meditate in His temple.   Psalm 27:4

Genesis 1 reveals the beauty of the Lord and that His temple is open to us through the path provided at great cost. As we accept this, His perfection and beauty is released to creation through each of us.

What does this mean in everyday terms? The final blessing of the traditional *Amidah* prayer (1st Century CE) says:

> ...for by the light of your countenance you have given
> us, Oh Lord, a *Torah* of life, loving kindness and
> salvation, blessing, mercy, life and peace.

Genesis 1:1 shows us this light, this countenance, and unlocks the *Torah*. This is the heartbeat that sustains life and all of creation. To align our heartbeat with this is to become what we should be. The message shows us how to begin to read the book – the *Tanach* and the Messianic writings known as the New Testament – with an open heart so as to learn how this may be walked out day by day:

Our voyage is complete, but the journey has only just begun. What we sought from the book of books at the opening to this study we have indeed found: history summed up, the essence and crisis of existence grasped, the key and resolution supplied, a hint of the end. And all in four words.

"With the drawing of this Love and the voice of this Calling
We shall not cease from exploration,
And the end of our exploring
Will be to arrive where we started
And know the place for the first time."
            (T.S. Eliot, Four Quartets, Little Gidding, V)

Shma

T he Lord calls to Israel, and to the nations, to hear Him There is an urgency to His call. "Shma, O Israel":

> Hear, O Israel! The Lord is our God, the Lord is one.
> And you shall love the Lord your God with all your heart and with all your soul and with all your might
> Deuteronomy 6:4–5

Can we so hear and can we so love?

In the beginning is a declaration of who God is. This enquiry has sought to decode the opening words of Genesis according to strict rules and subject to tough tests. We have applied neither the telescope to look at physical creation, nor the inward eye to examine our inmost parts. Instead we have used the magnifying glass to search out what the opening words actually say to us, avoiding noise and conjecture as far as possible. Our journey has led us deep into the Creator's heart for His creation. The heartbeat of creation is the Creator's sacrificial loving kindness to make relationship with Him possible. Creation beats with this heart.

From four words and sixteen letters a universe has emerged: the nature and purpose of creation. In the beginning, everything that was necessary was said. His opening words tell us of the moral order that is inherent to creation from the beginning. Here is the glory of God, the expression of the Creator in creation, the "here I am" of the one God.

If we dare to look clearly and consistently, then the puzzles, hidden-ness and mystery of His opening words, and the contradictions and disagreements in our understanding, are all resolved. There is one rhythm. In the beginning was the rhythm of His heartbeat established.

What we have found is not like a mysterious message in a bottle, tossed into the seas to be picked up by chance on some distant shore: one of many mysteries and puzzles cast abroad in the world today to distract us. This message is placed in the opening words of the book of beginnings. It demands our attention and contains a threefold call: to knowledge, to action, and to the prophetic.

If the Bible is the word of God, then from its every line we should anticipate the overwhelming experience of being engulfed by that which is far greater than us. This enquiry is an invitation to stand at the edge and to risk that full force. There is a time to move beyond safety. What we have found in the first great wave of Scripture is hidden, but it is not secret.

On the Day of Atonement *(Yom Kippur)*, a traditional prayer is proclaimed, which says in part:

> The Messiah our Righteousness has turned away from us, we are shaken and can find no-one who can justify us.[149]

We may be shocked; we may be shaking, but we have found that He is not far from us. His own sacrifice brings Him close to all who will seek Him, even amid the ruin of the world.[150] In Him we can have hope.

This enquiry has combed through the first four words of Genesis in great detail and with the utmost care. It has examined the foundational meaning of various Hebrew words and forms by looking at their root. The many Scriptures and Hebraic studies cited have informed our search and in turn our understanding of these has been informed by what the opening words tell us.

At the outset, we deliberately set the bar of our expectations unreasonably high. Our expectations have been more than fully met.

---

[149] Eliezar Kalir, op.cit.

[150] Rabbi Sa'adia Gaon (lived 882–942 CE, Egypt and Holy Land) says that, although the person making this prayer may be shocked and shaken, the Messiah as son of man has already carried his burden. Forgiveness will be found and a new creation achieved through the fulfilment of Isaiah 53.

The first verse in the Bible poses the core question of our existence that is pursued throughout the Bible. Beneath the plain text of the first verse is the key that provides the answer to that question and which opens the door to a deeper comprehension of all that follows. The entry code reveals to us the basis of relationship between Creator and creation and the dynamic that is unfolded in the Bible. The answer both confronts and potentially releases each of us. It reveals both His heartbeat and our founding reality. What we have found is that everything – everything – from first to last, from physical cosmos to internal world, and throughout all creation centres on this.

The Lord has encoded all this in less than a handful of words. Indeed, the first word of the Bible on its own tells us of the essentials of creation. The third word tells us of the Creator. In combination, the opening words build and confirm the form for relationship between the Creator and His creation and the rhythm for all creation.

Given the way it is constructed and hidden, this key is intended for use by those with a deep love and knowledge of the *Torah*. It tells how the Lord will, in the words of the *Alenu* prayer, perfect the world through His hidden healing and concealed perfection. It provides the basis on which we can go to the Law, the Prophets and the Writings that comprise the three parts of the *Tanach*. The code, with its constituent components, meets the criteria set out in the opening chapter. Hidden within the opening words of the Bible is a message that meet the ten tests of being: inclusive, precise, coherent, robust, appropriate to context, powerful, relevant, elegant, connected to actual events, and unique.

The entry code is uniquely fulfilled by one specific person, event and sign, and no other. That person, event and sign are the most controversial in history and its centre. Finally it becomes simple. This is God with us through the son who Father God eagerly introduces to us through His first words. And then the Word became flesh and dwelt among us. This is who He is. And we are made in His image.

The conclusions and overview reached by this enquiry differ from those normally found in Hebraic thinking, because that is where close examination of the text has inescapably led. What is opaque is finally resolved by using the key provided in the beginning. There comes a time to uncover our eyes and behold wonders from the word of God.

The code is no game for it tells us that there are consequences to our decisions. No acceptance of covenant or its fulfilment entails no basis for relationship with God, no secure foundation for our lives and no release of His creative power toward us. Instead, we are separated from the Creator and have no breath of the knowledge of God. The key to the alternative path is missed. What He wants for us, and offers to us, is life. As the pinnacle of creation, our rhythm should reflect the Creator's heartbeat. This is life, for we are created for His glory (Isaiah 43:7).

May each reader be prepared to be encompassed by the first great wave from God's word, to hear and experience and proclaim what His opening words say. In and from the beginning there is a covenant and a covenant sacrifice. The very name of the Creator spoken in the beginning tells of His heartbreak and provides His covenant oath to us. To read the opening of Hebrew Scripture with understanding is to hear His heartbeat and to be called to respond.

> Rejoice greatly, O daughter of Zion!
> Shout in triumph, O daughter of Jerusalem!
> Behold your king is coming to you;
> He is just and endowed with salvation,
> humble and mounted on a donkey...
> Zechariah 9:9

Appendices

Appendix A: The Hebrew alphabet

Appendix B: The twenty-six components

Appendix C: Objections

Appendix A: The Hebrew alphabet

א	Aleph
ב	Bet
ג	Gimmel
ד	Dalet
ה	Hey
ו	Vav
ז	Zayin
ח	Chet
ט	Tet
י	Yod
כ or final ך	Kaf
ל	Lamed
מ or final ם	Mem
נ or final ן	Nun
ס	Samech
ע	Ayin
פ or final ף	Pe
צ or final ץ	Tsadi
ק	Kof
ר	Reish
ש	Shin
ת	Tav

Appendix B: The twenty-six components

Step One: The act of creation

a)

בראשית ברא אלהים את

Genesis 1:1; the first four words

ב not א

Bet not *Aleph*

b)

בראשית

ברא   *bet-reish-aleph*   *Barah*

Creation

Step Two: The burning house

c)

בראשית

ראשית   *Resheith*

Beginning

d)

בראשית

ראש   *reish-aleph-shin*   *Rosh*

Head; first, cornerstone, sum, destitution

e)

בראשית

בית   *bet-yod-tav*   *Beth*

House, temple

f)   בראשית

ברית   *bet-reish-yod-tav*   *Berit*

Covenant

g)   בראשית

אש   *aleph-shin*   *Esh*

Flame, foundation

Step Three: Family

h)   בראשית

בר   *bet-reish*   *Bar*

Son, pure, grain of wheat

i)   בראשית

שית   *shin-yod-tav*   *Sheth* or *Shet*

To appoint, Eve's son Sheth; the good gone bad; shameful clothing.

j)   בראשית ברא

יתב   *yod-tav-bet*   *Yetib*

To sit (in judgement)

Step Four: Broken connections

k) בראשית

ברש   *bet-reish-shin*   *Berosh*

Tree

בר א שי   *Aleph*

Beginning, link between God and humanity

l) בראשית

שי   *shin-yod*   *Shay*

Gift of homage

ש   *Shin*

Divine power or corruption

m) בראשית ברא

תבר   *tav-bet-reish*   *Tebar*

Brokenness, the consequences of judgement

ת   *Tav*

Completion; the end

Step Five: The arrow

n) ברא   *bet-reish-aleph*   *Barah*

(second) creation

Step Six: The Creator's heartbreak

o)   **אלהים**   *Elohim*

      אל   *El*

Names of God

p)   **אלהי**   *aleph-lamed-hey*   *Ala* / *Ela* plus
                                                                yod

Name of God (singular).   My oath or consequences of
breaking an oath; my strong tree

      מ   *Mem*

Concealed

q)   **אלהים**

      אלם   *aleph-lamed-mem*   *Ilem*

Sheaf of wheat; person bound into silence; entrance to the
temple

r)   **אלהים**

      הי   *hey-yod*   *Hy*

Lamentation or wailing

s)   **אל הי מ**

The Lord whose suffering is concealed

or

The Lord who cries out in woe from amid the sacrifice

Step Seven: The sign

t)   את   *aleph-tav*

First and last, everlasting

u)   את or אות   *aleph-vav-tav*   *Owth*

Sign

Step Eight: Hidden names

v)   בר א שית ברא אלהים את

The son I appoint to creation (*or* to creating), *Elohim*, the first and the last

w)   בר א שית בר א אלהים את

Son, son of man, son of God, the first and the last

Step Nine: The barest breath

x)   בר א שית בר א אלהים את

The spare *alephs;* the barest breath of the presence of God

y)

רוש	or	ראש	*rosh*
ברוש	or	ברש	*berosh,*
תבור	or	תבר	*tebar*
אולם	or	אלם	*ulam*
הוי	or	הי	*hoy*
אות	or	את	*owth*

The absent *vavs*. Our role.

Step Ten: Recovering the question

z)   ראשי   my head

    אשי   my fire, my foundation

    ברשי   my tree

    אלהי   my oath, my consequences of breaking
                 an oath, my [strong] tree

The *yods*.   What   is   the   Lord's;   the   hand   of   God

Appendix C: Objections

Some possible objections to the logic and overall thrust of our argument are set out below, together with responses.

This is no more than an assembly of misleading bits and pieces. Really it is all random and means nothing.

In that case, chance draws a long bow in the beginning. These bits and pieces just happen to: occupy the critical ground at the start of the Bible; connect together in the way described; reveal the twin themes and pose and answer the core question of creation; meet the tough tests and criteria set out at the start of this enquiry; and point to the key event and person and sign in history. The key happens to fit precisely and uniquely.

To place a moral purpose as the driving force for all of creation, with humanity as its centre, is absurd, a projection of religious mythology.

Mere myth or a communication from the Creator about the purpose of creation? We have shown that this can be tested and, if the latter, has direct consequences for each of us. On both counts our findings are unlike, say, the popular modern concept that there are an infinite number of universes with an infinite number of Elvises etc. Such an idea is not testable but itself projects a myth of nihilism.

The words of the Bible have come down to us over the millennia through countless human hands, so it's pointless examining them in minute detail for a message from the Creator.

The Dead Sea Scrolls demonstrate the success of generations of Hebrew scribes in exactly preserving every detail of Scripture. As with the example of DNA, the Creator of life knows how to compress, transfer and secure vital information against every disruption. If He wishes to communicate with us through detail in the *Tanach* He will.

You can't prove that God exists.

I can't, He can; but He speaks only to those who are prepared to listen.

The method or the conclusions are unfamiliar.

That the method used leads to the conclusions stated is, indeed, unexpected. That is the point.

The vowel pointings in my printed text of Beresheis (Genesis) would not allow some of the readings you have extracted.

The vowel pointings are a later addition to the text in order to help the reader. Traditional *Torah* scrolls do not contain them and nor is the *Torah* discussed in such terms in the *Talmud* or commentaries.

The Talmud and eminent Jewish sages are frequently referred to and used to support parts of the argument, but the conclusions differ dramatically from theirs.

Correct. In scientific and other enquiries, normal procedure is to build on existing information and methods to reach new results that may go beyond the prevailing wisdom and resolve difficulties or lacunae. We draw on Judaic sources to inform and develop our understanding of various passages, words and letters and to demonstrate that we are not imposing an extraneous perspective on them. This does not bind us to conform to the conclusions of those sources (whose views vary greatly). That would negate the process and point of enquiry.

You have read backward from a selective interpretation of some words and passages in the Tanach.

Exhaustive survey of the first four words of Genesis has identified a range of words and concepts within that text. Those words and concepts have not been selected by us, and we have pursued every one without focussing on some and ignoring others. We have then looked to see what the *Tanach* tells us about these and how they are used. This provides the broader Biblical context for understanding what is being said. Inevitably, there are different views about how to interpret various passages. By comparing different Hebraic sources and fitting the different elements together, a picture is obtained which is coherent and consistent:

i.   internally

ii.   with the base text of Genesis 1:1, and

iii. with established Hebraic understandings of particular words, concepts and passages from the *Tanach*.

The whole is more than the sum of the parts.

You refer to Western philosophers but contradict their position.

Correct. Western philosophy, and its roots in Greek philosophy, make God unknowable, except as a reflection or attainment of the human mind (a perspective that has worked its way into both Judaism and Christianity). However, the Creator is not far from us and He makes Himself known to us. That is the point made in the first verse of Genesis.

This is all just speculation.

Speculation is guessing with little or no basis or intellectual rigour or method. Our conclusions are based on a stringent methodology, followed within strict limits. This lets the Hebrew Scripture speak to us, rather than reading in a chosen meaning. The consistency, coherence and robustness of what emerges are a check against possible speculation. As in any discussion, this is not to say that doubt or uncertainty can be eliminated.

The findings are another attempt to subvert Judaism and destroy the Jews.

On the contrary, our conclusions reveal the realisation of the hope of Judaism and the fulfilment of Israel's unique role. The way they are encoded shows these conclusions are aimed primarily at those who love the *Torah*.

You have misread the dualities in the entry code. They warn against the very claims you make.

In that case, we have a problem posed by the code – the divide between Creator and creation – without a solution. Neither Israel, nor any segment of humanity, can take on the role of a perfect sacrifice from God. The code of Genesis 1:1 would leave us without hope. The key would open the door to an unpleasant dead-end.

However you twist it, your argument involves denying the one God and thus the basis of the Torah and Talmud.

Not accepted. The core concept is of God as unity (*echad*) and unique Creator supreme over all creation. We do not depart from that. As noted in step six, Hebraic writers widely recognise that *echad* does not rule out some form of plurality within the God-head.

The analysis uses some short words that rarely occur in the Hebrew Bible. Some are not even Hebrew. The meanings you build on are forced and speculative.

The basis of our method was set out at the outset. We only use those words that can be found within the Hebrew letters of the first four words in the Bible and in the spelling and sense that they can be found in the Bible. This includes some Aramaic and Chaldean words that would have been familiar to people living in the late Biblical period (probably earlier) as well as to later students of the Bible.

We do not use extra-Biblical spellings or meanings and we do not change the order of letters or look at the beginning or ending of words or substitute one letter for another similar looking or sounding letter. Nor do we calculate the numerical value of groups of letters or make comparisons on that basis. Our rules are stricter than those normally applied in such enquires within the Hebraic tradition. For this reason, and the other four reasons stated in the opening chapter, our method is rigorous. Further, if the components that are based on short or scarce words are excluded from the analysis, the same composition still emerges.

Flawed or bad methodology has been used to project backward from that well known event and person and sign onto the opening words of Genesis. The message produced, together with its apparent internal logic, is an illusion.

In that case, it should be possible, by using flawed or bad methodology, to generate alternative 'illusions' from the first four words of Genesis: messages which are equally robust and coherent, equally align with the rest of the *Tanach*, and pass the other tests we apply, but are divorced from the meaning and implications of the entry code.

If your argument is correct, why hasn't it been made before?

As Scripture itself makes clear, there is developing or changing understanding of Scripture over time: everything is beautiful in its own time. The Messianic writings have conveyed the message for nearly two millennia, since its fulfilment.

Some findings are interesting but the argument goes way off course.

In that case, the erroneous parts of the architecture we have constructed should be easy to remove or correct. However, the inter-locking and complimentary nature of the components discussed means that many pieces of the jigsaw puzzle would have to be removed before the message could be drastically changed. Running through the results of our enquiry are the twin themes of the gulf between the Creator and creation and of the Creator supplying a bridge between them through His sacrifice. These twin themes act like a watermark that cannot be eradicated.

The code you discuss should be read as high-level allegory, myth or parable. It may contain a truth at some level, but not 'the truth'.

The message so carefully placed in the opening words denies the validity of a relativistic perspective which sees many, alternative truths but no single truth. Instead, the code concerns the truth that underlies all, the foundation of relationship with the absolute Creator. It is either absolute truth or it is false.

The code does not deal with the problems of pain and suffering or explain evil. It is incomplete as an answer to the core questions of existence.

The code shows how the Creator has provided to us what we most need, not what we think we most need. It reveals how God is engaged with His creation and how this is the basis of our hope amid pain and suffering. The foundation and goal of creation lie in relationship with the Creator. Evil is that which detracts or leads away from this and from our responsibilities toward others and the rest of creation. Relationship cannot be based on the absence of pain or suffering or evading responsibilities.

The message is so high level, it is no help in everyday life.

The message brings hope to those who can receive it. Understanding the nature and basis of relationship with our Creator provides our foundation for living and the means by which He can pour out His grace upon us. The entry code provides the starting point.

More copies of this book may be ordered from:
http://creationsheartbeat.blogspot.com or http://www.biblejolts.org

Breinigsville, PA USA
19 April 2010
236393BV00001B/18/P